TRELOAR'S

One Hundred Years of Education

Win

Local Studies Collection

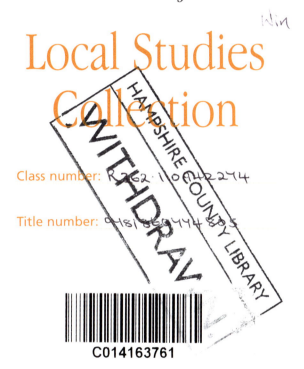

Class number: R 362·110942274

Title number: 0481860444805

Hampshire
County Council

CL81 7/02 10k

Lord Mayor Sir William Purdie Treloar, 1906-7.

TRELOAR'S

One Hundred Years of Education

JANE HURST

Phillimore

2008

Published by
PHILLIMORE & CO. LTD
Chichester, West Sussex, England, PO20 2DD
www.phillimore.co.uk

© Jane Hurst, 2008

ISBN 978-1-86077-480-5

Printed and bound in Great Britain
by Ashford Colour Press Ltd

CONTENTS

LIST OF ILLUSTRATIONS

Frontispiece: Lord Mayor Sir William Purdie Treloar, 1906-7

Acknowledgements

Thanks go to Gladys Moynihan, Angela Thomas, the families of J. Butler-Kearney and Rob Small, Arthur Beaumont, the Treloar Trust, the Hampshire Record Office (ref. 47M94), The National Archives (ref. ED 32, ED 62), the *Alton Gazette and Alresford Advertiser*, the *Hampshire Chronicle* and many others for their help and permission to publish photographs.

Illustration Acknowledgements

The illustrations are reproduced by kind permission of the following, to whom any application for use should be made: Treloar Trust: Frontispiece, 1, 3-11, 13-15, 17, 21-4, 36, 44-5, 48, 50, 54, 56, 57-8, 60, 63-5, 67-71, 73, 77, 80, 82, 87-9, 91-6, 100-1, 103, 105-6, 108-9, 111-16; Hampshire Record Office: 16, 20, 25-8, 30, 32, 34-5, 37-9, 41; Gladys Moynihan: 31; Hampshire Museum Service: 33; Phyll Wood: 42; Edna Mussell: 43; J. Butler-Kearney: 46-7, 49, 51-2, 69; *Hampshire Chronicle*: 53, 75-6, 78, 90, 104; Rob Small: 62, 74, 81, 83; *Daily Express*: 67; Kimroy: 72, 85, 98-9, 102; R.A.F. Odiham: 79; *Alton Gazette*: 86; Arthur Beaumont: 97; Bobby McDonnell: 107; Graham Photography: 110; Private collection: 2, 12, 18-19, 55.

Former Lord Mayor Sir David Brewer, 2005-6.

FOREWORD BY ALDERMAN SIR DAVID BREWER, CMG, FORMER LORD MAYOR OF LONDON, 2005-6

Sir William Purdie Treloar was a great visionary; he was also caring and very practical. That Treloar's is thriving 100 years on is testimony to his vision.

Providing the disabled in society with treatment and training to enable them, ultimately, to support themselves, was a new concept in the early 1900s—as were some of the fundraising techniques employed by Lord Mayor Treloar to fund his vision. Over the years, both have gained common currency, whilst the challenges facing disabled people remain.

This book charts the evolution of the education and training element of the Lord Mayor Treloar Hospital and College. Today, with Treloar School, Treloar College, the Treloar 'Moving On in the Community' programme, and a growing number of associated outreach activities, Sir William's vision is still at the cutting edge, enabling some of the most disabled young people in Britain to take control of their lives and dare to dream.

It was my great pleasure, and that of my wife, Tessa, to embrace Treloar's Centenary Appeal as the beneficiary of my appeal when I was Lord Mayor of the City of London exactly 100 years after Sir William. We have seen the work of Treloar's at first hand over many years and never cease to be amazed at the dedication and skill of all the staff, and the bright energy of the students. Our Mayoral year brought us much closer to this very special place which is set, I know, to continue its great work for at least the next 100 years.

This book charts times of significant social, medical and educational advances; it also records the development of a great organisation. I hope you enjoy it, and if you can support the Trust in continuing its work, I can assure you that help will be very warmly received.

Alderman Sir David Brewer, CMG

INTRODUCTION

This book has been written to mark the centenary of Treloar's. In fact there are several centenaries to be celebrated. 1906 was the year Sir William Purdie Treloar became Lord Mayor of London and began his appeal for money in order to found the Hospital and College. The next year the 'Lord Mayor Treloar's Cripples' Home and College' Trust (soon after called the Lord Mayor Treloar Trust) was formed and the premises were acquired. In 1908 the first children arrived at the Hospital and the first boys at the College.

The medical side of the Treloar story has been covered in Gladys Moynihan's excellent volume, *The Lord Mayor Treloar Hospital and College*, which was published in 1988 and is still available. Hence this book looks mainly at the aspect of Treloar's that might be termed, in its broadest sense, educational. The main sources for the story are the Trustees' Minutes, Annual Reports, school magazines, newspaper articles and Ministry of Education files, as well as memories of staff and students. Actual words have been used where possible, and so terms that were current at the time are included, even though they may not now be politically correct. No apology is made for this.

Something that may confuse Altonians and other locals is that the Hospital site was always referred to as being in Alton although it was actually in the parish of Chawton until the early 1930s, when the boundary was changed. As the book is following the establishments that were run by the Lord Mayor Treloar Trust (later called the Treloar Trust), it is concerned with the Hospital and College up to 1948 and then the College and Schools to the present time. The term 'Treloar's' has been used as a shorthand for the Hospital and College and, after 1948, for the College and Schools.

As must always be the case when trying to cover 100 years of history, more information has been left out than put in. Hence apologies are offered for omitting your favourite memories and pictures.

CHRONOLOGY

1843   Birth of William Purdie Treloar.

1906   Sir William Treloar became Lord Mayor of London and launched the Lord Mayor's Little Cripple Fund, which raised £60,000.

1907   The Lord Mayor Treloar's Cripples' Home and College Trust formed. The Alton Military Hospital Act of 1907 transferred the site of the Princess Louise Military Hospital at Chawton, near Alton, to the Trust.

1908   The first patients for the Hospital and boys for the College admitted.

1913   The Queen Alexandra League formed.

1919   Hayling Island site opened.

1948   The National Health Service took over control of the Hospital but not the College.

1953   The Lord Mayor Treloar College moved to Froyle.

1956   The school for handicapped boys opened at Froyle.

1965   The Florence Treloar School for Girls opened at Holybourne.

1969   Princess Alexandra opened the Newton-Davis Hall at Froyle.

1978   The Lord Mayor Treloar College and Florence Treloar School amalgamated.

1984   The Duchess of Gloucester opened Gloucester House at Holybourne.

1987   Prince Charles opened the Traill Centre at Holybourne.

1997   The Princess Royal opened Heywood House at Froyle, and the School and College were restructured.

1

The Cripples' Home and College

On 13 October 1907 a postcard was posted in Alton saying: 'The Lord Mayor visited Alton on Sat. last to inspect the Camp that is to be the Cripples' Homes and Orphanage.' As so often happens, the local information was not quite correct.

The visitor to Alton was indeed Sir William Purdie Treloar, Lord Mayor of London. He had been born on 13 January 1843 in the family home in Holland Street, Southwark. After leaving school, William entered his father's business, which became Treloar & Sons, dealing in 'cocoa nut fibre matting', carpets, linoleum, Chinese matting and rugs. When he was 22, William married Annie Blake—a marriage that lasted 44 years. Although not a person who liked the limelight, Annie supported William in everything he did. The couple were to have no children of their own, and it is possibly because of this that Lord Mayor Treloar Hospital and College was founded.

Reluctantly at first, William Treloar began to take part in civic affairs, becoming an alderman in 1892 and Sheriff of London seven years later. He was President of the National Sunday League, which fought for the opening of public museums, art galleries, concert rooms and parks on Sundays. When the Boer War broke out, William worked with Lord Mayor Newton collecting money to enrol and equip the 1,800 men of the City of London Imperial Volunteers and despatching them to Cape Town. For this achievement, both men were knighted.

In 1892 the *Daily Telegraph* appealed for money from its readers in order to fund New Year hampers for the 'crippled children of the Metropolis', with the Ragged School Union supplying a list of children. The next year Sir William became involved in the scheme, and eventually up to 7,000 hampers were being distributed every Christmas. At the same time Children's Banquets at the Guildhall in London were started and several thousand children would be fed and entertained each year.

Sir William Treloar became Lord Mayor of London in November 1906 and he and his wife, Annie, decided that the position might enable something permanent to be done to help 'London's cripples'. They were both aware that

1   *Sir William and Lady Treloar, 1906-7.*

few of these children went to school and believed that what was wanted was 'a cripple institution, which shall do its best to cure the suffering and then train the helpless cripples to become useful members of society'. Sir William had been told by experts that the cost of such a venture would be £60,000 (roughly equivalent to £4 million today), and so £60,000 was the amount he was determined to raise. £12,000 came from the Queen's Fête at the Mansion House, which was opened by Queen Alexandra, and from this beginning grew the Queen Alexandra League, which collected money for Treloar's over many years.

When his ideas became known, Sir William received lots of suggestions and advice including some from Dr Kimmins of Chailey. Dr A. Eichholz, of the Board of Education in Whitehall, thought that the 'scheme is a crying necessity for London', and Mrs E.M. Burgwin, who worked for London County Council (LCC), reported that there were about 2,000 crippled children in London requiring education but only 1,500 of these were attending or upon the rolls of the LCC Special Schools. She agreed that they would benefit from attendance somewhere where treatment and educational training were combined, but felt that only a few would really profit from skilled or technical training. It was suggested that the institution should be certified by the Board of Education in order that the London Education Authority might pay for children under 16 and might allow children over 16 to hold scholarships. Gradually, Sir William formulated his plan—in his own words:

The best possible way of helping cripples to regain health, and to become useful, is to remove the tuberculous-afflicted children to purer air, and to add to medical care and attention a course of manual training, to fit them to gain a livelihood.

Having raised the money, Sir William now turned his attention to finding a site for his scheme. Luckily, Mr Hall Richardson of the *Daily Telegraph* knew of some empty buildings at Chawton, near Alton. They had formed a Military Hospital Camp receiving wounded soldiers during the Boer War that had been built with money collected by the *Daily Mail*. In June 1900 the *Hampshire Herald* described the site as 'a beautiful park-like piece of land' lying 'on the slope of a tree-crowned hill which will protect the hospital from northerly and easterly winds'. It continued by saying that 'the subsoil is chalk, the water excellent and the new light railway to Basingstoke skirts the property on one side, permitting of a railway siding being built immediately in the rear of the wards' and ended, 'the air at Alton is delightful'. The buildings had become known as the Princess Louise Military Hospital but, with the ending of the Boer War, they had become redundant.

Sir William lost no time in visiting the Secretary of State for War, Mr Haldane, as an Act of Parliament was needed to convey the property from the War Department to the recently formed Lord Mayor Treloar's Cripples' Home and College Trust. The Act, known as the Alton Military Hospital Act, 1907, was rapidly passed. Having secured his premises, Sir William appointed two people whose hard work and dedication were to be so important to the future of the project—Dr Henry Gauvain as Resident Medical Officer and Miss Janet Robertson as Matron. Between them, their loyal service to the Trust amounted to over 60 years.

2   *The Princess Louise Hospital.*

3 *The Forest School.*

Right from the start, Sir William had thought that 'the Institution should be curative and educational'. When showing people around the site, he explained:

> We hope to have in the wood at the back of the Governor's quarters a Forest School, in which the children will receive such education as their bodily strength will permit. You will notice that we have an ample space for playgrounds and recreation gardens. We are going to use ten acres on the western side as a kitchen garden and fruit garden, and we shall have a large poultry farm in that part of the estate also. On the eastern side, close to the entrance gate, will be the technical school [the College], the senior lads' quarters, and their recreation room. Boys will be admitted to this section from the Physically-Defective Schools and other agencies all over England and Wales for the purpose of giving them a sound education in a useful trade, and so equip them to earn their own livelihood.

4 *The Aviary.*

5   *The Poultry Farm.*

The open-air school was built on the lines of the Forest School at Charlottenburg, near Berlin, and a winter schoolroom was also provided. As well as a poultry farm, provision for pig keeping was made and a large aviary was built and filled with British birds, the majority of which were birds of the district. Sir William hoped that this would 'be the means of awakening the minds of the children, transposed in the majority of cases from mean streets and sordid courts, to a knowledge of natural history'.

During 1907 and 1908 'little alterations', as Sir William called them, were made to the pitched pine Army buildings.

> The ward buildings consist of two main blocks of ten wards each. The wards are grouped round a semicircular corridor which affords a ready means of access between them. Each ward is self-contained, on one floor only, and has windows on three sides, and a considerable air space all round it. The blocks are so placed that each ward has windows facing open country to the South, so that the patients receive the full benefit of the sun at all hours of the day, a most important factor in the successful treatment of tuberculous cases.

At the end of each ward was a glazed enclosure which could easily be converted into an open veranda.

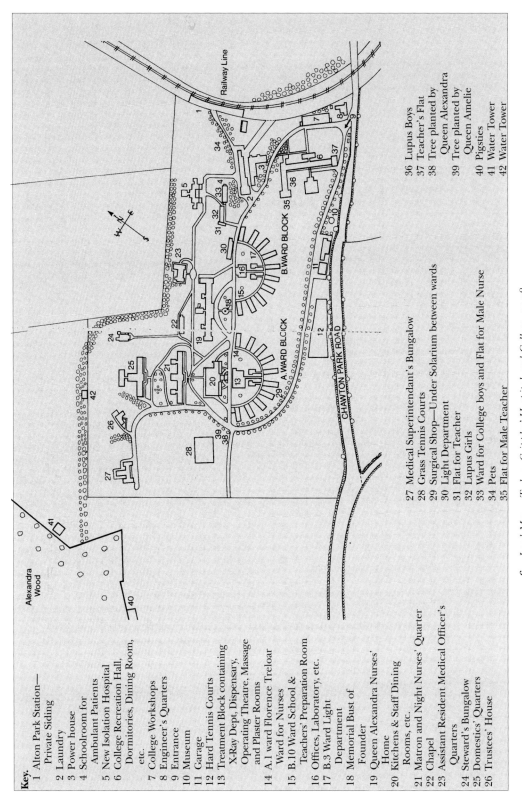

Key.

1 Alton Park Station—Private Siding
2 Laundry
3 Power house
4 Schoolroom for Ambulant Patients
5 New Isolation Hospital
6 College Recreation Hall, Dormitories, Dining Room, etc.
7 College Workshops
8 Engineer's Quarters
9 Entrance
10 Museum
11 Garage
12 Hard Tennis Courts
13 Treatment Block containing X-Ray Dept, Dispensary, Operating Theatre, Massage and Plaster Rooms
14 A.1 ward Florence Treloar Ward for Nurses
15 B.10 Ward School & Teachers' Preparation Room
16 Offices, Laboratory, etc.
17 B.3 Ward Light Department
18 Memorial Bust of Founder
19 Queen Alexandra Nurses' Home
20 Kitchens & Staff Dining Rooms, etc.
21 Matron and Night Nurses' Quarter
22 Chapel
23 Assistant Resident Medical Officer's Quarters
24 Steward's Bungalow
25 Domestics' Quarters
26 Trustees' House
27 Medical Superintendant's Bungalow
28 Grass Tennis Courts
29 Surgical Shop—Under Solarium between wards
30 Light Department
31 Flat for Teacher
32 Lupus Girls
33 Ward for College boys and Flat for Male Nurse
34 Pets
35 Flat for Male Teacher
36 Lupus Boys
37 Teacher's Flat
38 Tree planted by Queen Alexandra
39 Tree planted by Queen Amelie
40 Pigsties
41 Water Tower
42 Water Tower

6 *Lord Mayor Treloar Cripples' Hospital and College, 1908.*

2

THE FIRST YEARS

On 12 September 1908 the *Hampshire Chronicle* reported:

> … the Lord Mayor Treloar Cripples' Home and College commenced its beneficent work on Monday [the 7th], when the first batch of the future inmates arrived. Four nurses had gone to London to bring the 15 children to Alton Station, where they were met by Sir William and Lady Treloar. Four carriages were waiting to take them to their new home … the sun shining brilliantly in a cloudless sky.

Tuesday's *Daily Telegraph* had given an account of the departure from Waterloo Station, describing the parting of mothers and children. It was understood that groups of 15 children at a time would be arriving at the Hospital twice a week for the next six weeks. At the end of October the first consignment of boys left London for the College. They were said to come from all parts of England, including five boys from Birmingham.

In early November the College Master (F.W. Salt) reported to the Trustees on the Tailor's Shop and the Leather Shop. The poultry farm was already stocked with 304 birds and the piggeries had one boar, four sows and 29 small pigs. By the end of November the College boys had formed a football team and a Dramatic and Literary Club, which had provided a 'really good entertainment' with Sir William and friends attending a rehearsal.

Sir William explained the philosophy of education in the Hospital and College in the *Book of the Queen's Fête of the Queen Alexandra League* of 7 and 8 December 1909:

> Whilst the children are under treatment, a part of the scheme ensures that their education, where possible, may not be neglected. There are two spacious schoolrooms—the winter schoolroom, which has easy access from the wards, and the forest school. Besides this I hope that those children who of necessity have to remain in bed will receive such an education as they are capable of assimilating. At the same time it is never forgotten that the primary object to be obtained is the cure of the

7   *Leather bag making.*

8   *Football.*

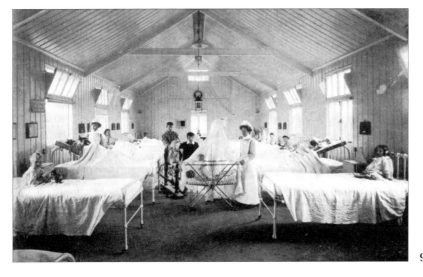

9   *A ward.*

disease, and the education of no child is allowed to interfere with the medical treatment, but rather by adding to the little one's interest in life, it is made an adjunct to promote a cure.

The aim of the College is, as I have said, to give such technical instruction to cripple boys of 14 years of age, and upwards, as will enable them to earn their own living. The College is situated close to the entrance gates of the estate, and the buildings comprise the school house, technical school, the concert room, and the library. In the school house there are two large dormitories and 25 small cubicles. The cubicles are allotted to the monitors who have, by reason of industry and good behaviour, earned this privilege … each boy makes his own bed, and scrubs the floor of his own cubicle.

The technical school is divided into three large schoolrooms. One of these rooms is used for the carpenter's shop, where all the splints, extensions, etc., are made for the children in the sick wards. I hope in the future that the College boys will be taught to do all this work. The indoor trades taught at present are leather bag making, fitted case making, boot repairing and cobbling. Although the boys have only been under instruction three months, remarkable progress has been made in the various trades, and I had the honour to present to H M the Queen a really beautiful brief bag made by the boys, and presented through me to her with an expression of their gratitude for Her Majesty's great and sustained interest in Alton.

The day and concert hall is a very spacious and lofty room about 50ft. square. Here, when the day's work is done, the lads play various games. Quite a number possess musical ability. Some play the piano or organ, others stand round and sing. A few boys have joined the village church choir.

10 *At lessons.*

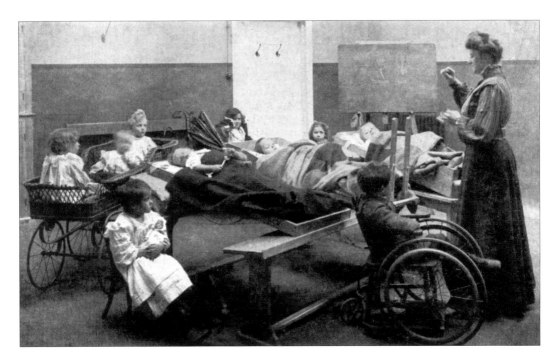

11   *Spinal cases at school.*

The object of the College is to build these young lads up physically, whilst at the same time equip them with a skilled trade and, above all, to give them a manly tone in their outlook upon life, and to teach them not to whine over their physical deficiencies, but to face the battle of life with confidence and with courage.

Sir William was keen that children should receive religious instruction in the faith of their parents. He had engaged nurses belonging to different religious denominations so that, in case of sudden sickness or emergency, a child would have the comfort and sympathy of someone of his or her own faith.

In July 1909, less than a year after achieving their goal, Lady Treloar died. This must have been a great loss to Sir William, who said himself that she 'took so much interest in every detail of my plans and my work'. After this their adopted daughter, Florence, became more involved in the running of the Hospital and College, accompanying Sir William on his visits and eventually becoming a Trustee.

By March 1910 it was reported that the railway sidings to the site were finished and awaiting inspection by the Board of Trade. These allowed coal to be brought straight into the grounds. When the inspector visited a month later, he noted that 'a small platform for the use only of the patients' had been erected. This was known as Alton Park and it was here that the many visitors to the Hospital and College arrived, including Queen Alexandra and Queen Amélie of Portugal in 1912.

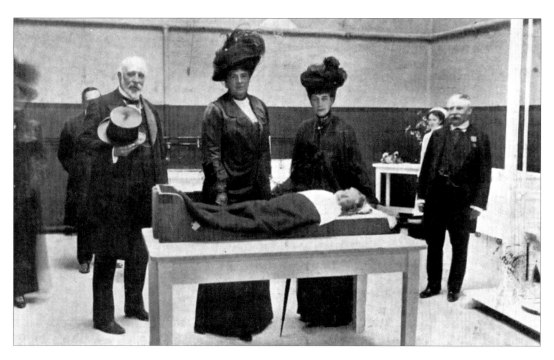

12   *Queen Alexandra and Queen Amélie at the Hospital.*

Sir William, with the Lord Mayor and his Sheriffs, visited on an important mission in May 1911—the opening of the Mansion House Museum. Earlier,

> a suggestion was made to the boys that they should build for themselves a museum … and in their spare time a substantial and suitable building was erected. It is octagonal in shape, 18 feet in height and 23 feet in width. All the work connected with the excavations and foundations was carried through by the boys themselves, under the guidance of the Estate bricklayer.

The foundation stone was laid in 1910 by Lady Knill as Lady Mayoress of London, and the building was formally opened on 20 May 1911 by the succeeding Lady Mayoress, Lady Vesey Strong. The building was to house collections of animal and plant life from the neighbourhood of Alton as well as various donations.

Many years later, Henry Gauvain, the Resident Medical Officer, recalled the early Hospital education:

> Nature is a great healer; rest, fresh air, sunlight, good food, hygiene, are all readily available, and all fully utilised, and I would add to these occupation with a specific object. Realising this from the opening of the Hospital, we started a school in which manual training played an increasingly important part. The effect on the children's mentality and happiness

13   *Queen Alexandra Wood, in the Hospital grounds.*

was immediate and startling. We commenced with one governess and later, for financial reasons, had to dispense with her assistance, but I was so convinced of the value of occupation and education of the children that when we had lost our governess we carried on with the voluntary help of the nurses alone. This work attracted the attention of the Board of Education. There followed a visit from Sir George Newman [Chief Medical Officer to the Board of Education] and Mr. Lloyd George, then Chancellor of the Exchequer, who, recognising our needs and seeing how they could be met immediately, instituted Hospital Schools which, certified by the Board of Education and staffed by approved teachers, could earn both medical and educational grants.

As well as meeting all these visitors, Gauvain had more mundane worries. In October he told the Trustees that a suitable anthracite stove was urgently needed for the winter schoolroom, as the children were exposed to undue cold and suffered from chilblains.

Ever open to new ideas to promote the Hospital and College, Sir William had a film made. On 2 December 1911 it was reported in the *Hampshire Observer* that 'Sir William Treloar … realising that Londoners will not readily subscribe to a hospital that is not in its midst, has brought the hospital to London by means of the cinematograph.' It was shown at 105-7 Charing Cross Road and included scenes of children drilling in the winter schoolroom, children going to the Summer School in the woods, the Museum built by the College boys, College boys making their own beds and Sir William refereeing a football match.

By the time Henry Gauvain wrote a report in March 1912, he could say:

> at Alton all children receive such education as their condition permits, and on discharge commonly have not only made up for the loss which their enforced absence from school has engendered, but often, because of the care taken with their education, are perhaps even in a better position than if they had attended school uninterruptedly.
>
> In our College, crippled lads are received from the age of 14 to 18 for technical training in an <u>occupation suited to their limitations</u>, for a period of three years, and on discharge are able to take up remunerative and self-supporting occupations, to their own gain and that of the community.

The College Workshops taught leather work, cobbling and tailoring. There was also an instructor in drill.

Sadly, not all the children who came to the Hospital recovered. Chawton parish register records the following burials of young patients for 1911:

23 March	Lionel Lock, aged 8
17 April	Hilda Pritcher, aged 10
22 November	Norman Victor Allen, aged 6

The Hospital was in Chawton parish during its early years and so burials took place there. In 1929 the Trustees decided to make an annual grant of £5 to Chawton Church for the proper maintenance and care of the graves of children buried in Chawton Churchyard and to consider immediately the

14 *Winter School.*

question of suitable gravestones. This suggests that the earliest burials may not have had stone memorials.

In 1913 the education at the Hospital became formally recognised. At a Trustees' meeting on 19 November, the Chairman reported that the Hospital had been certified by the Local Government Board and the Board of Education. The Trustees had engaged four teachers who had been approved by these authorities. The cost of the scheme would amount to about £800 a year but Treloar's would receive about £1,600 a year from government grants. Sir William pointed out that the Trustees were now enabled to take cases from county councils, which had the power to pay the cost of the boys' maintenance and treatment.

A month later it was reported that the regulations for school teaching had now been inaugurated by the Trustees (in accordance with the rules of the Board of Education) and the appointment of the following teachers was confirmed:

on 19 May 1913	Miss A.N. King	at £100 p.a.	
on 16 June 1913	Miss O.K. Cook	at £65 p.a.	
on 1 November 1913	Miss A.E. Lee	at £165 p.a.	(Head)
on 1 November 1913	Miss O.G. Champress	at £120 p.a.	

The Trustees resolved that the daily work in the School would be five-and-a-half hours 'at such times as best suited the medical work' (as decided by the Resident Medical Superintendent) and that a whole holiday would be given on Saturdays. The teachers' holidays were to be taken during June, July, August and September—one month each, as arranged. They would also have one week at Easter and one week at Christmas. Some of the other salaries paid by the Trustees were: Dr Gauvain, £600; Mr Salt, £250; Miss Robertson, £110; and the Rev P.E. Teulon (the Chaplain) £100.

15   *View from the north-west.*

3

The First World War

Within a few weeks of the start of the First World War in 1914, Sir William was thinking of taking '6 or 8 little Belgian children, who have been crippled in the War', but nothing seems to have come of the scheme.

By December 1914 the Trust's auditors had prepared a statement of account for the Board of Education. Sir William estimated that the grant would amount to about £1,200, which, after deducting expenses for teachers' salaries and materials, would leave about £600. He reported that Dr Gauvain had been sanctioned to appoint another assistant teacher. During the nine months ending 30 September 1914, 'books, apparatus, and other materials for purposes of Instruction' cost £140 5s. 9d. and salaries were £363 13s. 1d.

At a meeting of the Trustees in March 1915, the Chairman read the following extract from a letter from the Board of Education:

> The present accommodation for teaching purposes is not altogether satisfactory. A considerable improvement would be effected if it were found possible to provide, by means of open-air balconies leading from the Wards or otherwise, further accommodation which could be used for teaching purposes, and which would enable the children to be grouped more suitably from the educational point of view. I am to add that the Board would be prepared under the Finance Act, 1911, to consider the advisability of making a contribution towards the capital expenditure thus incurred.

But Mr Leonard Stokes, the architect, reported that 'to meet the requirements of your Board fully, it would be desirable for us to entirely rebuild. Plans are now being prepared for that purpose, and when they have advanced further I hope to submit them to Sir George Newman and your Board for their criticism or approval.' It was thought that a temporary measure giving balcony accommodation on the north side of the wards would cost £380. The Board of Education learnt with interest that the Trustees were considering rebuilding but they thought that it was very doubtful if it was worth spending so much on any temporary improvements.

16   *A drawing made by a patient at Alton.*

The First World War meant a reduction in male employees as they gradually joined the forces. Sir William's Founder's Day speech of 1915 had to be made at Mansion House, London, as the London South Western Railway Company had cancelled the special train that was due to take everyone to Alton because of 'Military requirements on the Line'.

In July 1915 the *Alton Gazette* reported on the 'Hampshire Day' held at the Hospital:

> those children who were able to get about were found in the schoolrooms being taught the ordinary work of an elementary school, while others were being trained in various handicrafts under skilled instructors, basket making, mat making, and all kinds of fancy needlework and useful crafts. Not only are the children cured, but they are educated and in many cases taught valuable and useful occupations. There were many samples of the work done on exhibition to prove that it is not a mere superficial knowledge that is given, and the education of the children is also recognised by the education authorities in the payment of annual grants.

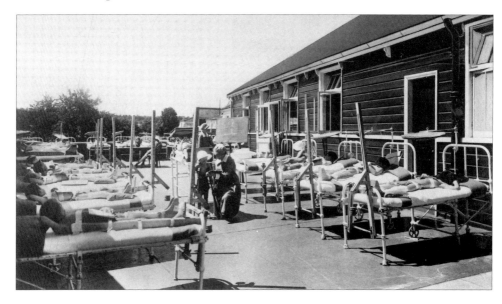

17   *A lesson taking place in the sun.*

18   *The dedication of Naval Memorial Wards at the Hospital, 31 May 1917. The escort were men of the Fourth Destroyer Flotilla who fought in the Battle of Jutland.*

In the Annual Report for 1915-16, Dr Gauvain wrote that the educational work of the Hospital had attained a high standard and that all children capable of deriving benefit from instruction were educated by specially qualified school teachers. The work of the Institution had won warm commendation from the government and, in the report of the Medical Officer to the Board of Education, the Hospital was referred to as 'representing the best type of technique in England at the present time.' All children above the age of five, whose condition permitted, received three hours' systematic instruction daily.

Dr Wilson of the Board of Education inspected the Hospital School in January 1917. She expressed her complete satisfaction but drew Dr Gauvain's attention to the fact that the children were not supplied with glasses and she was of the opinion that, for the proper performance of their lessons, the eyes of each child should be tested and spectacles provided where required. Gauvain felt that this could be expensive but that it would be of great benefit to the children and to the College boys.

19   *The College boys at dinner. The flooring came from Treloar & Sons.*

20   *College boys playing cricket.*

4

The College

The College year was now divided into three terms and new boys only arrived at the start of one of them. On leaving, one of the most serious drawbacks that the College boys suffered was the lack of knowledge of elementary business principles. To remedy this, evening classes at three levels were formed. On Monday, Wednesday and Friday evenings between 6 and 7 p.m. from September to Easter, the boys had instruction in book-keeping 'and other minor business details' as well as 'general intelligence' lessons. These were taken by Miss Lee, the Headmistress, Miss Hibberd and Miss James. Miss Lee was paid 5s. an hour and the others 3s. 6d. an hour. Tuesday evenings meant choir practice for the boys, and Thursdays were set aside for 'kit repairs'.

In October 1916 Henry Gauvain reported that the arrangements for the College School were proving highly satisfactory, meeting a very real need, and were much appreciated by the boys themselves. Mr Wenmoth, the Assistant Charge Master, organised games and other activities, and a neat but serviceable uniform had been introduced.

The College boys' apprenticeship was limited to three years and during this time they were encouraged to invest any savings. On leaving they were granted money 'to make a start on their own account'. Instruction started to be given in 'elements of Hygiene, the practice of Thrift, and preparation for the responsibilities of civic life'. The boys' weekday routine was:

6.30 a.m.	'Reveillé'
6.30-7.30 a.m.	Dressing, making beds, attending to dormitories. (There was no domestic assistance.)
8.00 a.m.	Breakfast and attending to their pets
9.00 a.m.	The bugler sounded 'Fall in'—to work
12.30 p.m.	Dinner and rest
2.00 p.m.	Work
5.00 p.m.	Tea, recreation and lessons
8.00 p.m.	Supper
9.00 p.m.	Muster for evening prayers
9.15 p.m.	To their quarters
9.30 p.m.	'Lights Out'.

21   *College boys in the gymnasium.*

The boys' recreations included the use of Indian clubs and dumb-bells, football, cricket (with matches played against local teams such as Alton Brewery, Alton Church Lads' Brigade and Alton Postmen) and the keeping of pets such as rabbits, bantams or pigeons—whose houses they built themselves.

In the College's Report of 1916, it was said:

> the attempt to introduce the Public School spirit into the College has proved most successful, and it is encouraging to find that many boys look upon the College as their second home. Every Bank Holiday a number of old College lads visit the scenes of their training. Matches are played between them and the present pupils, and there is also a close connection between the boys who have left and their instructors. Friendships made in the College have been maintained outside, and for some time past a number of College lads who are in business in London have formed a Club among themselves. They meet from time to time, and those who are able to do so have started a cycling section.

The College Boy Scouts were inspected at Aldershot by Sir R. Baden Powell in February 1917 and were said to be the first troop of crippled Boys Scouts in the country.

After running the College evening classes (known as the College Continuation Classes) for a year, Dr Gauvain explained:

> the education of these lads has in many cases been gravely, and sometimes completely, neglected. To rectify this an evening school was founded last winter, designed to meet their peculiar requirements. Three classes are held—elementary, intermediate, and advanced—and

22   *The College workshops.*

CASE AND BAG MAKING

BOOT MAKING AND REPAIRING

TAILORING

the instruction given includes reading, writing, and simple arithmetic, English history, book-keeping, business-letter writing, invoicing, etc., and English literature. This intensive and special instruction has proved of very great value and is most keenly appreciated by the lads themselves.

The literature evening was a decided success, the boys being very interested in the books they were reading; their arithmetic and writing showed slower but steady improvement.

Interestingly, a Board of Education Inspector's report sheds a different light on the first day-time College lessons (known as College School) to be introduced:

At first there was a great deal of opposition from the boys themselves and just a little "feeling" from the trade instructors who were inclined to resent the boys being withdrawn from their trade work for this general instruction. Within three months, however, this was all overcome and all have acknowledged the great benefit obtained. The discipline amongst the boys at first seemed hopeless and they played off all the tricks they knew, such as rolling the ink bottles down the desks, filling their pockets with gravel and at intervals throwing it over the floor. They seemed to have no sense of honour and glibly lied to the teachers. A remarkable change has come over the whole school due to the tact, keenness and careful management of Miss Lee and her two assistants. The discipline is now all that could be wished and the boys are really keen and anxious to get on.

The Inspector also described how the classes were arranged:

Since January 1918, proper systematic courses of elementary instruction in the 3 Rs have been arranged. The boys are classified according to standard ability into three sections. The lowest contained 18 boys and they were instructed daily from 9.00-10.30 am. The next section contained 17 boys and they were instructed between 10.45-12.15 pm. The top section (all over 16 years) with 15 boys received instruction daily from 2.00-3.00 pm. Great thought and care has been given by Miss Lee to drawing up a suitable syllabus and she personally examines the work done every fortnight.

The boys' work included business letters, book-keeping and reading newspapers and magazines.

Miss Lee, the Headmistress, was very highly thought of. Dr Gauvain reported that 'the Board of Education regards this Hospital School as a model one, and invariably sends to us authorities contemplating the establishment of Hospital Schools for physically defective children, to study and imitate our methods.'

The boys' instructors were Mr Sayers for leather bag and casemaking, Mr Wenmoth for tailoring and Mr Graham for boot making. Mr North was the drill instructor and supervised Games, while Mr Aitken, the steward, taught the commercial aspects of trade. In the evenings there were various activities such as a Debating Society, Glee Club, Hobby Club, Games and lectures.

A letter from the Board of Education, dated 6 January 1919, stated that they were prepared to recognise the College under the Special Schools Regulations. The Trustees completed and dispatched the necessary forms and the College was certified under the Elementary Education (Defective and Epileptic Children) Act, 1899, for the accommodation of 50 boys as from 13 January. The Board was also prepared to recognise the courses of instruction for students over 16 years of age under the Special School Continuation Courses Regulations as from 1 April 1918 and provisionally agreed a grant under those regulations. The timetable and curriculum were approved and the Board added that the College would be regarded as a separate institution from the Hospital and its school for administration purposes. The first grant the College School received was £252 towards salaries and £113 towards materials.

5

HAYLING ISLAND

The opening of a seaside branch of the Hospital had long been a dream, and in 1918 a house and 60 acres of land had been purchased at Sandy Point on Hayling Island. Many alterations were needed to the site, but on 11 September 1919 the first patients were transferred there, arriving by motor ambulance. They were met by Sir William and Miss Treloar, Dr Gauvain and Miss Robertson.

In March 1919 Henry Gauvain sent a letter to the Board of Education telling them that 'we open our Seaside Branch at Hayling Island in June' and that they would, in due course, be applying formally for the recognition of that branch as a Hospital School. 'We propose to appoint two teachers, who will be responsible for the education of 50 patients.' Three months later Gauvain wrote that Hayling Island was of an experimental nature and might not be open in the winter months. The proposed timetable for the Hayling Island School was:

9.30-10.30 a.m.	Arithmetic, writing, reading or drawing
10.30-11.00 a.m.	Nature study, geography, reading, history or general information
11.00-11.45 a.m.	Breathing, physical exercises, games, paddling, fishing, or bathing
1.30- 2.45 p.m.	Handwork
2.45- 3.00 p.m.	Singing
3.00- 3.45 p.m.	Breathing, physical exercises, games, paddling, fishing, or bathing.

Some of the lessons had a seaside theme, for example History included 'Historical Sea Stories', 'Our Victories at Sea' and 'The Lives of Nelson and Drake'.

The Board of Education visited the new establishment in December and they found 40 children in the large ward, six in a small ward and four in cubicles, with Dr Gauvain visiting twice a week. The school there was to be run as part of the Alton Hospital School and was under the supervision of Miss Lee, the Headmistress, who was to visit once a fortnight. Four additional teachers had been appointed—two for the Nursery Class at Alton and two for Sandy Point. The new school was certified as a Special School for Physically Defective (Tuberculous) Children as from 11 February 1920.

23   *Patients at Hayling Island.*

PAVILION VERANDAH.

SEA BATHING.

REFRESHMENTS AFTER BATHE

NATURE STUDY ON THE BEACH.

SCHOOL ROOM.

A LESSON IN GARDENING.

24   *Lessons at Hayling Island.*

6

BETWEEN THE WARS

Following the First World War, Treloar's was affected by changes in education. The Burnham Scale for teachers' pay was approved by the Board of Education and the teachers at Alton and Sandy Point were paid according to this from the start of 1920.

The patients who came to the Hospital also began to change and several county councils asked about the terms for admitting children. This was probably in consequence of the 1918 Education Act, which required local authorities to make special educational provision for all disabled children who needed it and were judged capable of benefit. The Board of Education said they would not in future make grants for children received through local education authorities.

The 1920-1 Annual Report announced that there were now five 'schools' being run at Treloar's: College Continuation Classes, the College School proper, the Seaside School at Hayling Island, the Hospital School and a Nursery School. Treloar's was said to be 'the first institution of its kind to be approved as a Nursery School for children up to the age of five years'.

After a visit in June 1921, the Board of Education Inspector wrote:

> Miss Lee is now head of practically 3 large schools, viz: Alton Hospital (240 on books), Alton College (50 on books) and Hayling Island branch (50 on books), but her salary is only £312, i.e. less than many an Assistant's in a much smaller organisation. The assistant teachers are also paid less and I think work harder than in most Special Schools. I gathered that the Managers would be willing to increase the scale if any word to that effect came from the Board of Education. I think a letter of commendation should be sent and if possible a hint about salaries.

It is not clear if the hint was dropped or taken.

The children's parents could visit them between 2.00 and 3.30 p.m. on Saturdays and Sundays, and on Bank Holidays they could come in the morning between 10.30 and 12.00 and in the afternoon between 1.30 and 3.30—on presentation of a visiting card. The College was closed for a week or ten days

25   *The Chapel.*

at Easter and Christmas and for the month of August. Those who did not go home had to contribute about 10s. a week towards their maintenance.

In the Hospital School ingenious apparatus was used whereby 'even tiny patients immobilised on spinal stands in apparently uncomfortable attitudes' could receive instruction, and breathing exercises were given in every ward morning and afternoon. Letters home were written once a week by all children who could. Several older children corresponded with subscribers and pupils in public schools. Forty girls enrolled in the Girl Guides, and all kinds of handiwork, such as leather work, rug making, needlework and picture tinting, was done.

At Hayling Island the Board of Education allowed the timetable to be varied so that bathing could take place during the hour before high tide. Here the education was practical as well as instructive, partly designed for the purpose of cultivating and training the powers of observation. There were rambles on the seashore for combined Geography and Nature Study lessons with the gathering of all kinds of specimens. The children kept wind, weather and tide charts and had a rockery and gardens. Handiwork was done on the shore when possible, especially the making of shell pictures. Organised games and short plays also took place. Later, a new schoolroom was set up, and in 1928 Miss E. Colver presented the children at Hayling with a statue of Peter Pan for erection in the garden.

26 *Lessons outside.*

27 *A lesson in basket making.*

28 *Open-air school. Note the teacher's uniform of overall and cap.*

The College boys were entered for the elementary book-keeping examination of the National Union of Teachers and, out of class, they organised lectures and entertainments, took part in debates and produced a College Magazine.

In 1923 Sir William celebrated his 80th birthday and entertained 1,000 children at the Crystal Palace. There was a circus and tea, and each child received an autographed picture of Treloar and three new pennies in an envelope. Sadly, before the year was over, Sir William had died. A giant wreath of roses was sent from Alton— 365 blossoms from the 365 patients. Money was invested so that its dividend would be sufficient for the annual upkeep of Sir William Treloar's grave-stone in Shirley churchyard and 'In Memoriam' notices were to be annually displayed on 6 September, the anniver-sary of his death.

29 *Handicrafts in the open.*

Sir William's death brought to an end his great personal involvment in the running of the Hospital and College. The whole of the establishment's development since he and his wife first had their vision for helping 'London's cripples' had been guided by his hand and many of his own words have survived in his speeches and in newspaper articles. From now on, the records are mainly Minute Books and Annual Reports that, naturally, lack the warmth that only the 'Bold Baronet Who Couldn't Grow Old' could give them.

The next year's Annual Report showed that the passing of Sir William was not the only change. A difference had been noticed in the types of cases admitted. Improvement in the school medical service and more accommodation for non-pulmonary tuberculosis, especially in London, had resulted in the condition being detected and treated earlier.

In 1925 Mr Harper, the Secretary of the Hospital and College, called at the Board of Education to discuss the admittance of non-tuberculous cripple cases from Portsmouth for orthopaedic treatment and other matters. As well as discussing this, the Board of Education asked for an assurance that the trade instructors would be engaged under written agreements. Mr Harper explained, 'Instructors of this type are not regarded by his managers as teachers at all. They are paid weekly wages at the usual trade rates. The men do not desire to come under the Superannuation Act and no deductions from their wages have been made for this purpose.' The managers were concerned that they might have to get 'people of a very different educational standard which would mean a very considerable increase in the expenditure incurred.' At this time, as well as the instructors, there were 13 teachers including the Head, Mrs Aitken (Miss Lee had married Mr Aitken, the steward), and they wore the uniform that can be seen in some of the pictures.

In the mid-1920s the Trustees approved the suggestion that the College Boys should take up allotments, using part of the land forming the sports field. Dr Gauvain (now Sir Henry as he had been knighted in 1920) proposed that the proceeds of any produce sold should be given to the cultivators. Tools worth £20 were bought and two labourers were employed to trench the ground two spits deep as it was decided that this would be too much for the boys. A series of lectures and demonstrations on gardening was arranged and wire netting put round the plots to keep out rabbits. The boys also acquired a wireless set and a Kodascope to show films.

In the Report for 1925-6, it was said that during the past year 590 children had been enrolled on the school registers. The opening of the orthopaedic wards was also mentioned, which had meant that a special curriculum had needed to be arranged to meet the frequent changes of pupils. There was now a day room for the teaching of convalescent patients, and these children had longer school hours and a wider curriculum, 'so keeping them occupied, and happy all day and better preparing them for their return to ordinary school life.'

The General Strike of 1926 found the College and Hospital well-stocked with steam and house coal. The only anxiety was about meat and groceries but their own van went to London three times a week to collect goods. As soon as the Strike started, a rigid economy in coal and light was enforced.

At the same time, the College boys on the vocational courses were having lessons in reading, geography, letter-writing, composition and dictation, arithmetic, geometry and book-keeping. Every term Mrs Aitken held a test and those who were fit moved up to the next section. In the workshops it was difficult to keep up with orders for goods. At the end of each term, reports on health by Sir Henry, trade work by the instructor, general conduct by Mr Aitken (the steward) and on instruction by Mrs Aitken were sent to each boy's parent or guardian and a copy to the Authority or person paying for him. 'This report has a very salutary effect on the boys themselves as they fear to have an adverse report.'

At the end of their time at Treloar's, the Steward arranged interviews for the boys with prospective employers and practically all of them obtained work. On leaving, they received a bonus in order to buy a set of tools. Many Old Boys who set up their own businesses would give College lads employment when they left.

In 1927 arrangements were made with the Committee of the Seaside Camp for London Boys, at Walmer in Kent, for those Treloar boys who were unable to go home for the holidays to go there for a fortnight. They would then spend the rest of the summer holiday at the College. When the boys returned from Walmer, the Camp Superintendent wrote to say that the College boys had won

30   *The gates to the Hospital and College.*

the competition for the best section for most of the days that they were there. 'They mixed freely with the other chaps and joined with them in their games ... while I hope it may have helped them they certainly taught us many lessons.' The boys were sent the Trophy Flag which was awarded to the section winning the highest marks for good conduct, smartness, cleanliness and efficiency. This was just the first of many such visits to Walmer.

31 *A class of ambulant children.*

The Annual Report that marked the 20 years since the foundation of the Hospital and College stated:

> the introduction of teaching in Hospital is one of the greatest benefits conferred upon the suffering child ... As a link in child education the Hospital School prevents gaps and broken chains which would otherwise necessarily occur ... the individual touch this special teaching affords is a very great advantage to the child, more especially to the dull or backward ones. The latter have very little chance in the big classes of the elementary school, or in the home, but the individual bedside teaching in Hospital naturally reveals the child's mind to the teacher, and many difficult stages are overcome ... To the very young children in the Nursery Wards, school is a very great attraction, and their little minds are unconsciously trained in a hundred ways.

The late 1920s were a time for considering the future of the College and Hospital and their buildings. The old timber wards were costing too much to repair, having been in use for about 30 years. The Trustees also discussed the extension of the College to include the training of crippled girls, but it was decided not to proceed with this. Instead they planned to extend the work of the Hospital and to convert the existing College accommodation into a new treatment area, ward and schoolroom for lupus and ambulant cases, and to erect a new building for the College on the field on the other side of the road, adjoining the railway line to Winchester. The architect was asked to go into the matter thoroughly and prepare sketch plans. The Board of Education Inspector recommended that the College boys had a 'quiet room', as there was only one large hall for recreation, general teaching and quiet study in the evening. It was also suggested that the boys had a sick bay so that they would not have to go into a children's ward for hospital treatment.

In 1928 Sir Henry reported that several teachers had left and it was likely that they would lose others. The reason was that at most hospital schools the teachers worked shorter hours and had higher pay—hence it was becoming

32 *A College workshop.*

increasingly difficult to select the best type of teacher. Gauvain felt that the Trustees should consider whether they would 'fall in with the majority of hospital schools and give shorter hours and a higher scale of pay'. Enquiries revealed that most hospital and special schools had two hours and 15 minutes teaching in the morning and two hours in the afternoon in accordance with Article 26 (3) of Grant Regulation No.19 for Special Schools, 1925. It was required that not less than seven hours per week was given by the teachers to preparation, in addition to the actual teaching hours. If such a change was made at Treloar's they would require an additional five teachers, and Sir Henry thought that it would then be unnecessary to give the teachers lunch or tea. The Trustees discussed the report but decided to take no action.

In the same year, Mr North, the College Master, reported that he did not think his health would permit him to continue working. He was then aged 60 and had been at the College since 20 June 1908. Sergeant Major Keeble replaced him as Housemaster and was responsible for the boys' recreation and out of work hours as well as supervising meals and the dormitories. Mr Aitken, the steward, was responsible for the working of the College. The College boys' library was overhauled and Edgar Wallace, the author, promised to present several of his books.

For some time Sir Henry Gauvain had been looking for suitable school desks and seats for the ambulant children when at school. Whilst it was easy to find them for those suffering from spinal disease, it was not so for those with hip tubercle and so he drew plans and had them specially made.

By 1929 it could be said:

> all children from the age of two years receive daily instruction, those proving lengthy cases being promoted by stages, according to ability. Children who evince marked ability are given every opportunity of progressing, while the dull, backward, and undeveloped child is given the advantage of unremitting individual attention, which proves a wonderful aid, and often apparent signs of mental defect mean only an undeveloped mind and brain.

Advanced handicrafts allowed boys

> who may be too old when discharged to return to school, to learn
> to cultivate a workmanlike attitude ... In general intelligence and
> resourcefulness a sick child often triumphs over the normal ... The
> introduction of teaching in Hospital has opened out a wide field for
> educational research and possibilities, apart from giving the child a
> healthy mind to fit a healthy body.

In order to mark the 21st anniversary of the College, the Steward proposed
a rally of old College boys on Whit Monday, 20 May 1929. He also suggested
that the College boys might have a badge on their blazers and enclosed a
design by a member of the teaching staff. The Trustees approved of the idea of
a badge but not the design as they thought there should 'be something more
applicable to the Arms of Sir William Treloar'. After the summer holidays, all
the boys were fitted with grey overalls,

> which gives them a workmanlike appearance and will protect their
> clothing. The new grey tweed suits for best wear were also used for the
> first time. Only first year boys and new boys are being fitted out with
> the new suits, so that it will take some time before the whole of the boys
> are in the same colour clothing. We are still using khaki drill suits for
> workshops and ordinary wear.

In the summer of 1929, while
trenches were being dug for the new
Hospital, the workmen unearthed
some pieces of pottery and a few bones.
The Steward had the opportunity
of submitting them to an expert, Mr
Heywood Sumner, who happened to
be visiting Alton. The largest specimen
was said to be a portion of the base of
a wheel-turned Roman platter. Other
fragments were a piece of a straight-
sided cooking pot and, probably, some
New Forest ware. The bones seemed
to be those of a red deer. These were
subsequently deposited with the
Hampshire Museum Service.

33 *Roman pottery found on the site in 1929.*

34   *The College cricket team.*

35   *A handicraft lesson.*

By 1930, final plans had been approved for the entire reconstruction of the wards. 'In the new buildings special provision is being made for schoolrooms, exhibition rooms, and dining and recreation rooms for ambulant cases; whilst more adequate and suitable accommodation is being provided for the teaching staff.' The Trustees thought that the education of a child was as important as its treatment. 'Not only is it essential to avoid any handicap educationally, owing to absence from school, but experience has proved that children respond more readily to treatment when being taught, and are happier for the school work.'

Changes were also taking place in the College. The ages for admission were altered from 14 to 18 years to 14 to 16 years. Leather work, which was a luxury trade, was suffering in the general depression, and because of this, more boys were choosing to go into the Shoemaker's Shop. At the same time, pig keeping stopped and the pigs were disposed of. In May the Trustees agreed to the provision of a small cricket pavilion to be built with material from a ward that had been demolished. The Secretary was asked to point out that it should only be in use during matches, 'as it was undesirable to provide a building where lads could get away for smoking and other purposes'!

An Inspector from the Board of Education visited in October 1931. He noted that the first two ward blocks were open and occupied and it was hoped that the third would be ready for occupation before Christmas. The teaching was on a 'double shift system' but it was suggested that this should stop when the new Hospital was completed. The teachers were working six hours a day but each child was only getting one-and-a-half-hour sessions. The ambulant boys were taught using the school hut and the ambulant girls in one of the wards.

36   *A veranda joining some of the wards.*

Mrs Aitken, the Headmistress, was ill and Miss Thompson was Acting Head. Mrs Aitken tendered her resignation in September 1933 after overseeing the completion of the new school buildings. She had been Headmistress since the Hospital School was formally recognised 20 years before and, sadly, she died only seven months later. The Trustees recorded that it was due to her that the Hospital School had enjoyed such a high reputation.

In March 1932 the Trustees were contemplating the appointment of a specially trained, fully certificated schoolmaster to take over the welfare work and education of the boys when they were not under instruction in the College workshops. Arnold Munden was eventually appointed in October and, at the same time, Major A.H. Ritchie became College Housemaster in place of Mr Keeble.

The Annual Report of 1932-3 stated that 'as a result of various experiments, we have come to the conclusion that these [College] boys are not capable of "deep" study. We are therefore trying to give them a variety of interests to broaden their outlook on education.' That year the College Magazine was composed, typewritten and duplicated by the boys and this led to typewriting being taught. Educational films were shown one evening a week during winter—the object taken being the British Empire—and a St John Ambulance class was formed.

By 1934 a new eastern block was ready. Below the wards were 'a dining-room with servery for ambulant patients, class-rooms, open-air and sheltered play-room, and hobby-room … In fine weather the ambulant children will be taught on a specially designed terrace outside the class-rooms. Adjacent is a head teacher's room, teachers' common-room, and necessary annexes.'

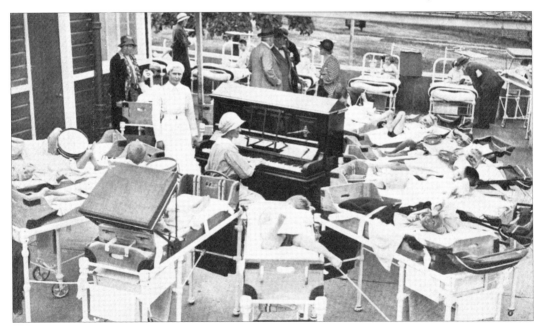

37 *The Babies' Toy Band.*

38   *A new schoolroom at Alton.*

The reduction in cases of tuberculosis of the bones and joints meant that new rules for admission had to be made: 'Boys and girls crippled from any cause whatever and who would be likely to be benefited by treatment are admitted up to the age of 16 years.' Other conditions treated included arthritis, infantile paralysis, osteomyelitis and deformity caused by rickets.

In 1934 it was said that the Hospital School hoped to develop special features. Records of good music were played 'to establish the beginning at least of taste … At a certain stage of convalescence the patients are able to assist in and accelerate their recovery by physical activities which include nature walks in the woods, specially planned physical training, and folk dancing.'

In the College School, education 'is chiefly concerned with making learning so attractive that the boys have an instinctive desire for it, and in this direction there is an encouraging amount of success' and good results were obtained in various exams. The College Dramatic Club presented two short plays in December and there were visits to the Cobham Air Circus, Alton Operatic and Dramatic productions and the Aldershot Tattoo, and there had been a day in London to visit the Zoo and see the annual Stock Exchange v. The Banks football match at the Arsenal Football Ground (played in aid of Treloar's).

The Board of Education visited the Hospital School in 1934. They were keen that, now the new Hospital was completed, the 'double shift system' should cease and that all children should go back to having at least two hours' instruction morning and afternoon. They thought that the teachers should

39   *School handicrafts displayed in the Exhibition Room.*

confine themselves to actual teaching and the necessary preparation for lessons, and not be responsible for ambulant children or other patients outside school hours. The managers protested that this would mean employing more staff, in response to which the Board suggested raising the fees. They also felt that medical treatment could be carried on at one end of the ward while instruction was going on at the other, children being withdrawn for treatment as required. The Board emphasised that it was important in an institution like Treloar's that the Head Teacher should be as free as possible from class teaching in order to supervise the overall running of the education and also to escort the many visitors.

After the 1936 visit from the Board of Education, Miss Thompson (the Headmistress) asked the Trustees if she could have a copy of the Board's report on the Hospital School. They decided that she should be informed that 'such reports were in the nature of confidential communications to the

Governors of the School' and she was only to have a general outline of the report. In fact the report, a copy of which can now be seen at The National Archives, was complimentary. It said:

> the nursing and medical staff were friendly and there was a spirit of give and take … There is a closer co-operation between the teaching and medical staffs. The Head Teacher consults with the Medical Officer, the Sister and the Masseuse in regard to the best forms of handwork for the patients so that the handwork is becoming a more definite and useful adjunct to treatment as occupational therapy.

The Ambulant Class consisted of about 25 children aged between eight and 16, and at the time of the Inspection they were trying out an experiment with wireless talks. The lesson was prepared beforehand and for the talk they sat in a semi-circle round the loud-speaker. Afterwards the lesson was discussed. The Inspector had also seen an after-hours woodwork class for the ambulant boys, which was run by the estate carpenter.

1937 was the year of the Coronation of King George VI. The Trustees agreed to present every patient and member of staff with chocolates in a special box bearing pictures of the King and Queen. The cost was 5s. 6d. for a dozen tins. It was also decided to buy sufficient bunting for the veranda at Alton and the pier at Hayling, but it was only to be used on Coronation Day and then put away for the opening of the new Hospital on 10 June by the Duke and Duchess of Kent.

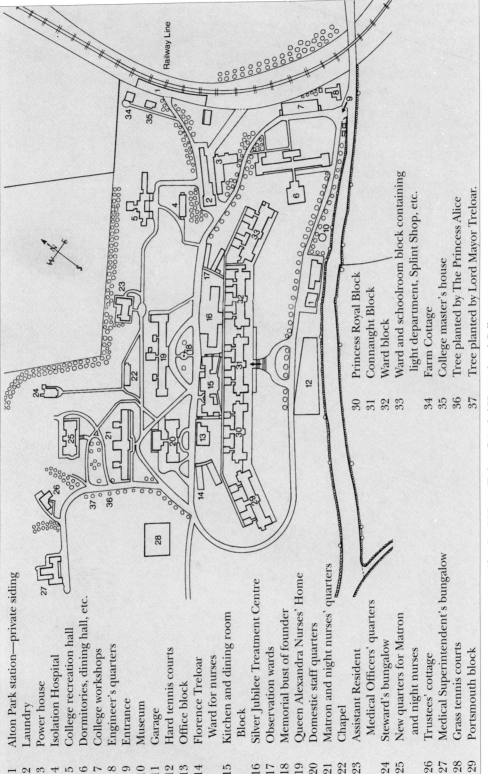

1 Alton Park station—private siding
2 Laundry
3 Power house
4 Isolation Hospital
5 College recreation hall
6 Dormitories, dining hall, etc.
7 College workshops
8 Engineer's quarters
9 Entrance
10 Museum
11 Garage
12 Hard tennis courts
13 Office block
14 Florence Treloar
   Ward for nurses
15 Kitchen and dining room
   Block
16 Silver Jubilee Treatment Centre
17 Observation wards
18 Memorial bust of founder
19 Queen Alexandra Nurses' Home
20 Domestic staff quarters
21 Matron and night nurses' quarters
22 Chapel
23 Assistant Resident
   Medical Officers' quarters
24 Steward's bungalow
25 New quarters for Matron
   and night nurses
26 Trustees' cottage
27 Medical Superintendent's bungalow
28 Grass tennis courts
29 Portsmouth block

30 Princess Royal Block
31 Connaught Block
32 Ward block
33 Ward and schoolroom block containing
   light department, Splint Shop, etc.
34 Farm Cottage
35 College master's house
36 Tree planted by The Princess Alice
37 Tree planted by Lord Mayor Treloar.

40 *Lord Mayor Treloar Cripples' Hospital and College, 1937*

7

THE SECOND WORLD WAR

Even before war was declared, preparations were being made. In September 1938 the Trustees considered the possible evacuation of children from Hayling and from various London hostels to Alton. Patients from Hayling seem to have been transferred at the end of 1939 on orders from the Ministry of Health. The three schoolrooms at Alton were turned into temporary wards in order to accommodate the 50 extra children, and the exhibition room was used as a schoolroom for the ambulant children.

When the Board of Education visited in 1940, they reported that adequate ARP (Air Raid Precaution) arrangements had been made. Some of the side wards had been prepared as gas-proof rooms for the small children who could not wear gas masks. Wheelchairs for the more severely crippled were kept on the veranda outside the College dormitory and a 'pusher' slept in the bed next to each boy needing a wheelchair. In the event of an AR (Air Raid) warning, all the College boys would go over to the Hospital 'winter playground', a building under the wards that was thoroughly protected by sandbags.

The Board also noted the Hospital ward routine:

5 a.m.	Patients washed, lavatory round
6.30 a.m.	Breakfast, lavatory round
7-8 a.m.	Making beds
8 a.m.	Hot milk given
8.30 a.m.	Prayers, Sister's morning round, play and rest period
10-12 noon	School
12 noon	Dinner
12.30 p.m.	Lavatory round
1-1.30 p.m.	Rest
1.30-3.30 p.m.	School
3.30 p.m.	Tea
4 p.m.	Lavatory round
4.30 p.m.	Bathings, treatments, etc.
6.15 p.m.	Supper

6.30 p.m.   Lavatory round
7 p.m.   Beds made, children tucked down for the night
7.15 or 8 p.m.   Lights out in the ward, time varied according to age.

Treatments took place between 8.30 and 10 a.m. and during school hours as necessary. The teachers' hours were 9.30 a.m. to 12.30 p.m. and 1.30 to 4 pm.

Despite wartime (or maybe because of it), the Inspector also checked the food and was given a specimen weekly menu. Below is Monday's:

Breakfast   Bread & dripping, cocoa.
Hot milk at 8.00 a.m.
Dinner   Beef stew & veg., egg custard, rice pudding & apricots, milk (chicken or bacon for special patients).
Tea   Bread & butter, milk, tea, eggs, jam, sweets, fruit, treacle, Marmite, etc., at Ward Sister's discretion.
Supper   Cocoa, porridge, or biscuits & bread, & milk, dripping.

After the visit, the Inspector's report read:

The exercise books of the pupils show that solid and successful work is done in English and Arithmetic, but it should not be forgotten that individual work in writing exercises from text books is only one aspect of these subjects, although one peculiarly suited to hospital conditions. The difficulties of group work with children in bed have not deterred some teachers from attempting play reading and even play writing in

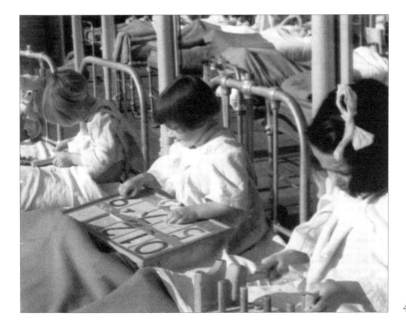

41 *Lesson time.*

42   *Filling sand bags.*

43   *Lessons on the veranda of the new Hospital.*

44   *A game of cricket on the recreational field.*

proper dramatic form. Drawing, painting, and design on paper are difficult for children in bed, but some pleasing sketching is done … the
staff are well aware of the dangers of allowing handicapped children to
leave a hospital, where their needs have been met by others, with a self-
ish outlook upon life; and they try to develop a spirit of co-operation
with others as well as of independence of mind so far as hospital conditions will allow. In doing so they are teaching their children one of the
most necessary and valuable of lessons.

The conclusion was that 'the high standard of all round efficiency has been
maintained at this hospital school which ranks as one of the finest in the country.'

On 30 September 1940 the war came a bit closer to Treloar's. About 40
incendiary bombs fell on land nearby but they were all extinguished. Pay-
ments of 2s. 6d. [12½p] per man per night were made for fire watching duties,
pulling down the heavy blinds in front of the wards, inspecting the blackout
and remaining on duty during the night. Later they received allowances from
the Alton Urban District Council for fire watching.

The war meant other changes. In the College, case making and fancy leather
goods making were given up due to a leather shortage. For the Hospital
patients, fine needlework was replaced by mending, patching and darning
of items for Treloar's. The boys as well as the girls knitted pullovers, helmets,
gloves, socks and mittens for the armed forces. The Hospital also provided 45
beds for the Emergency Hospital Scheme, which found beds for sick children
from bombed areas. As these patients were not getting any education, an
additional teacher was appointed. Treloar's was relieved of its obligation to
keep beds empty for these cases from 1 April 1945.

45   *Memorial bust of Sir William Treloar in front of the Queen Alexandra Nurses' Home.*

46   *A College classroom.*

47   *The College football team.*

In 1942 the College boys were moved out of their sleeping quarters, owing to the danger of being in the wooden buildings, and the open-air children's playroom was converted into a dormitory. 'Although there is definite overcrowding there have been no ill effects,' it was later stated.

The BBC visited the Hospital in 1943 and was preparing a script for broadcasting in South America about the treatment and education of the children. A year later the British Council wrote to the Trustees regarding the film 'Hospital School', which was about to be released in this country.

By 1944 there were only 25 boys in the College and the only courses were boot making and repairing and tailoring. The Trust Secretary was instructed to enquire as to the demand for places from local authorities and others who sent boys to the College. He also asked for suggestions about the trades which could be taught and government grants that might be available. A Government Inspector visiting in September 1944 reported that 'the centre at Alton would serve an extremely useful purpose as a Secondary School with a Technical bias for Cripples and … as another centre of the Younger Cripples from 14 to 19 years.' It was thought undesirable to have adolescents mixing with older men and so they did not want them sent to training colleges such as St Loye's at Exeter.

8

After the War

At the end of the war, the Hayling Island site was visited and found to be empty, having been occupied by the admiralty for the duration. In October 1944 Sir Alexander Maclean offered to fund the laying out of the grounds there, and it was hoped to be able to reopen, in a modified way, early in 1946. After a survey of damage it was realised that the coastal defences needed attention as well as the buildings. April 1946 saw the appointment of Miss Tennison as the teacher for Hayling and the re-opening took place a month later.

In 1945 the Trustees agreed to pay the teachers in accordance with the Burnham Report. This meant that they would be paid one increment (£12 a year) more than teachers in secondary or primary schools. The total salary increase created an additional expenditure of £1,500 that year. The teachers also received an allowance of £16 in lieu of meals. The new Education Act also changed some of the financial arrangements. The former capitation grant received for pupils not sent through education authorities was to be discontinued and replaced by a grant based on the cost of education, maintenance and treatment.

Discussions about the future of the College continued as boys were not coming forward in sufficient numbers. The Trustees proposed re-building the College and suggested possible new College courses—machine drawing, clerical, watch and clock repairs, pattern making and tool making, gardening, poultry farming and cooking.

Before anything was finally decided, news came of the proposed National Health Bill. The Trustees held a special meeting on 26 March 1946 to consider its implications. 'It was noted with concern that in its present form the Bill would destroy the Trustees' authority and that the endowment funds would be confiscated and used to pay the debts of other Hospitals including Local Authority Hospitals.' It was agreed to send out a letter to all the local collectors (who raised funds for Treloar's in different parts of the country) drawing their attention to the serious state of affairs. In it the Trustees said that they 'approve of the principles of regionalisation and co-ordination of Hospitals, but to achieve a more efficient and comprehensive Hospital system for the

48   *A College outing.*

country it is not necessary to confiscate the voluntary hospitals and destroy the voluntary spirit.' All collectors were urged to write immediately to their Members of Parliament and to their local press in protest.

A month later, a meeting was held about the future of the College. It was agreed that the College would be rebuilt to accommodate 100 disabled children, with 75 boys and 25 girls. Provision for possible expansion, if required, would be borne in mind. The new College was to be divided into two sections, one for children between the ages of 12 and 16 and the other for those between 16 and 21. It was agreed that trainees for the latter group should be admitted at such an age as would enable their training to be completed not later than the age of 21. They would concentrate mainly on vocational training but would also receive a certain amount of education. The younger group would form a Special School for Physically Defective Children with some vocational training. The scope of the Tailoring Shop was to be enlarged to include Dress-making for girls, and the Boot Shop was to continue training boys in Surgical Boot-making and Repairing.

The new College was to be built on the recreation field opposite the Hospital (between Chawton Park Road and the Watercress Line). The Trust Secretary was instructed to prepare a draft scheme to be sent to the Ministry of Education and the Ministry of Labour with an invitation to hold a conference at Alton.

Meanwhile the Hospital School continued as before. The Head Teacher requested new overalls for the teaching staff and it was decided that samples of available materials should be obtained in various colours to be submitted to Miss Treloar, a Trustee since 1920, for consideration. The Secretary reported that, so far, it had not been possible to obtain additional clothing coupons for the teaching staff. Consideration was also given to having an outdoor swimming bath near the tennis courts and the water tower. Nothing seems to have come of this suggestion.

The Trustees decided to appoint a Warden to be in charge of the College. The starting salary was to be £500 a year, with free residence when available. More than 120 applications were received and Lt Commander C.G. Brook was appointed. One of his first jobs was to make enquiries into watch and clock making and book-keeping with a view to preparing a curriculum for both, and it was decided to offer a course in gardening if any candidates wanted it. In the event, the watch making course was replaced by one in splint making. An evening Art Class and a Choral Society were started, and a Games Evening was organised with local German prisoners of war.

At the end of 1946, the Trustees agreed to appoint Messrs W. Curtis Green, Son & Lloyds as architects for the proposed new College buildings. Mr Green, the architect, offered to accept half the usual fee in the event of the Trustees being unable to proceed with the rebuilding of the College, which was to be classified as an 'Institution for Further Education and Training of Disabled Persons' instead of being a Special School. An alternative site in nearby Wyards Field was also considered. From this time the accounts for the Hospital and College were separated.

Almost 40 years after the opening of Treloar's, it was decided to make use of Sir William Treloar's coat of arms for the Hospital and College. This was already displayed on the board at the entrance. A little later, the Treloar Company of Girl Guides was enrolled and their Colours were dedicated.

In April 1947 it was thought that the College boys' uniform of a grey flannel suit should be replaced with a sports coat and grey flannel trousers. This was agreed 'on the understanding that the sports coat should be of a reasonable quiet pattern.' It was also agreed to adopt the Warden's suggestion that 'boys over the age of 16 be officially permitted to smoke when out of the College grounds on Saturday and Sunday afternoons and also when they have a mid-week cinema visit or similar privilege, subject to parent's consent'.

A few months later, the Trustees decided to make enquiries as to the possibility of finding an alternative site for the new College within two or three miles of Alton. In September Thedden House was inspected, and it was thought that the property, with about 50 acres of land, 'was worth consideration as an alternative for the new College site, the house on the site to be considered for use as a P.D.[Physically Disabled] School for the under 16's.' It was then found that the building was badly affected by dry rot, although work was in progress to remedy this and to make good the dilapidations caused by its occupation by the military during the war. In the event, there were too many disadvantages with Thedden and the Trustees agreed to keep looking around the area.

In the Hospital, some of the children had been busy working on an afternoon tea cloth that was sent to Princess Elizabeth as a wedding present. They received a letter of thanks.

49   *A College drama production.*

Changes were being made in the College. It was decided to take boys between the ages of 15 and 18 instead of 14 and 16. The Head Gardener had not welcomed the suggestion that he instruct college trainees in gardening, although he finally agreed—if a good second gardener could be recruited! The courses on offer in 1947 were surgical and bespoke boot making and repairing, tailoring, surgical splint making and gardening. A radio maintenance and repair course was also started. The work rooms, schoolroom and dormitories were renovated and brightly decorated.

In February 1948 the Trustees received a letter from the Ministry of Health. It said that the Regional Hospital Board and the Hospital Management Committee would have no power to conduct a Special School in the Hospital or the College, but they could arrange for the Special School to be carried on by the local authority or a voluntary organisation on Hospital premises. As the College was a separate activity, it was not thought to be transferable to the Minister of Health on the appointed day. The Trustees decided to prepare the case for dividing the funds in order to submit it to the Ministry and replied that they noted that it was agreed that the College buildings and land were not to be transferred but that they were 'apportionable', together with a share of the endowments in the Trustees hands, between the Minister and the Trustees. The Trustees added that as they would not be conducting the affairs of the Hospital after the 'appointed day', they did not wish to be responsible for the management of the Hospital School after 5 July 1948.

A little later, a letter came from the Regional Board inviting the submission of names of Trustees for consideration of appointment to the proposed Hospital Management Committee. All but Miss Treloar were put forward. There then followed several meetings between the Trust and the Ministry of Health about the apportionment of funds, premises, wages and insurances. From the funds held by the Trustees jointly for Hospital and College purposes, which amounted to about £838,000, the Ministry of Health was eventually prepared to agree an allocation of £250,000 for the College.

In November that year, the Trustees decided that it would be preferable for the Ministry to take over all the land and buildings, and then for the Trustees to pay rent for the College premises and recreational field until the College was housed or rebuilt on another site. In 1949 the Department of Education noted that the Treloar managers were only responsible for a training college of 30 boys. Hampshire Local Education Authority had accepted responsibility for the Hospital School and Ministry approval for the College Special School had been withdrawn when it closed on 1 April 1946.

During the Christmas term of 1948, the College Boys produced The L.M.T.C. Magazine. It gives a good picture of the workshops:

> BOOT SHOP. (18 Boys). We are now an official Surgical repair shop for the Ministry of Pensions, but I don't suppose that you would notice any difference. Mr Brand still has his cheery smile, and it is only in the confines of his office that an occasional worried look comes over his face as he tries to grapple with forms in triplicate.
> In the lulls of the boot shop hammering, you may be able to catch the strains of "Music While You Work" coming through the new partition wall, and coming through the door you will find the RADIO SHOP. (5 Boys). This has got away to a good start, and from it we hope to turn out a steady stream of first-class Radio Service Engineers. We welcome Mr Batchelor to the staff …
>
> TAILOR'S SHOP. (11 Boys). The old tailors' boards have been taken out, and tables fitted instead, in order to bring the shop more up to date. The shop will also be greatly improved by re-decoration, which is to take place very soon. Work has been at top pressure this term to cope with a rush of orders for new boys' suits, porters' uniforms, nurses' capes, etc. Mr Perschky and the boys are doing splendidly, but we must ask for patience from our clients.
>
> SURGICAL SPLINT SHOP. Two boys are at present working in the Hospital splint shop, learning this excellent trade under Mr Were.

The magazine also described some of the other College activities. There had been 'a very grand evening for November the 5th', two plays were performed—'Anybody' and 'There is So Much Good'—a number of books had been added to the College library and the College Quiz team was beaten by the Nurses' team by only one mark.

By the start of 1949 the Trustees were considering the purchase of Froyle Place, which was in the village of Upper Froyle, three miles east of Alton. After a satisfactory report from the surveyor, they decided to offer £18,000 subject to the approval of the local planning committee. In March there was discussion as to how the house and outbuildings could be used and it was agreed that a small administrative and appeals staff would work in Froyle Place itself. The Warden was asked to put forward recommendations as to layout, bearing in mind that training was to be provided for 50 boys with possible expansion to 100 boys. Contracts were exchanged on 11 July 1949 and a 10 per cent deposit of £2,000 was paid for Froyle Place and about 90 acres of pasture and gardens. Some furniture had also been bought at the contents sale. Completion date was 9 September and the Trustees decided to continue to employ the Head Gardener, two other gardeners and the caretaker.

The suggested future name was 'Lord Mayor Treloar Cripples' College', although Trustee Colonel Newton-Davis raised the question of the desirability of the word 'Cripples'. The College Warden was in favour of retaining the word and so it was decided to leave the matter in abeyance with the suggestion that the views of the boys might be obtained. At the meeting in November it was unanimously agreed that the name should be 'Lord Mayor Treloar College'.

The College Magazine dated Christmas 1949 recorded that Miss Treloar had visited for the celebration of her 80th birthday. A toast had been drunk and she had been presented with a copy of the Easter Magazine. 'Entertainment followed in the evening with two plays, the same ones, incidentally, which were acted at the Aldershot Drama festival and which were spoken of very highly by the Adjudicator there.' Further on, it was reported that the Radio Shop had built a television set and 'gramophone pick-up equipment with amplifier'. The boys had been to camp again in perfect weather and they were all looking forward to the day when they could move to Froyle.

At the start of 1950, plans were prepared for a dining hall, classroom and three workshops at Froyle. As this was not long after the War, a licence was needed from the Ministry of Works before work could start. Progress must have seemed very slow to the boys as the editor of the 1950 Christmas Magazine wrote that 'Froyle Place does not seem any nearer than it was when I came three years ago, when it was confidently predicted to be certainly not more than eighteen months before we moved. It has remained obstinately at that figure throughout my time here.' In fact, one group of boys did go to Froyle about this time. They were those on the Gardening course and they travelled there daily.

The Christmas Magazine also recorded the death of Herbert Perschky, the tailoring instructor. He was an old College boy, having been there in 1933, and 'knew every corner where a boy might slip out for a quiet smoke or some other guilty pastime but he never looked for trouble. During his "duty" nights he used to sit in his favourite armchair in the reading-room spinning those yarns of his which one never quite knew whether to believe or not.' In early 1951, there was another staff change when Frank Gasston was appointed as

50a and b   *The Gardening course at Froyle.*

Housemaster. There were changes, too, for the boys. They were to be relieved of cleaning up the workshops but they still had to wash up after tea.

By April 1951 five tenders had been received for the rebuilding at Froyle Place and all were in the region of £50,000. The alterations included the installation of central heating, creating classrooms on the ground floor, a housemaster's flat and boys' dormitories on the first floor and the caretaker's accommodation on the second floor. Ground outside was to be levelled for playing fields, the racquet court was to be put in good order to be used as a recreation room and the old theatre converted into an assembly hall.

Late in 1951 it was agreed that it would be desirable to have an open-air swimming pool at Froyle, but the plans were turned down by the Ministry of Education. In October 1952 the architect was asked to reconsider the provision of a swimming pool 'with the minimum requirements'; there would be no changing rooms or filtering plant and the water would come from the hydraulic ram near the River Wey. An indoor pool was eventually built in 1957.

A Trustees' meeting of February 1952 considered the question as to whether additional accommodation was required for College boys of the present age group or whether accommodation should be provided for younger ones. After discussions with the county council, it was reported that 'the most difficult educational problem in Hampshire was the provision of special school accommodation for spastics.' The Trustees, however, did not want to take in a single disability group.

Meanwhile Mr Brook, the Warden, had moved to Froyle Cottage, opposite Froyle Place, in October 1951. Soon after, he decided to leave and the Trustees advertised for a replacement. Francis Heywood, ex-Master of Marlborough College, was offered the post as from 1 May 1952. The salary was £1,500 a year, of which £300 was for expenses, and he was also to have free residence in Froyle Cottage.

51   *A College photo.*

52   *Old Boys' reunion, Whit Monday 1950.*

Coinciding with the arrival of the new Warden were changes to the College Rules and Regulations. It was agreed to alter the word 'crippled' to 'disabled' and Rule 9 was to read:

> Each boy on admission should bring serviceable clothing, ration book and medical card. The minimum clothing requirements are 2 pairs of boots, 1 pair of slippers, 1 tie, 3 shirts, 3 vests, 3 pairs of pants, 3 pairs of socks, 3 suits of pyjamas, 4 handkerchiefs, hair brush and comb and tooth brush. Replacements and additions will be supplied by the College free of charge except for the cost of footwear which is charged to the Authority and/or Ministry of Pensions.

53   *Francis Heywood, Warden 1952-69.*

54   *Froyle Place and the kitchen extension.*

All this time, meetings about the apportionment of the Treloar funds between the Hospital and College continued. As the situation became clearer, the Trustees bought more property—Froyle House (known as The White House), two cottages and 10 acres for a price of £10,000 and the Froyle Place Estate for £135,000. Froyle House subsequently became Trust offices with staff accommodation upstairs.

The 1952 Annual Report suggested that the College would move to Froyle early in 1953. It read:

> it will be strange and in some ways sad, after so many years as part of the Hospital, to see the College on its own, fending for itself outside the protecting walls at Alton. One can liken it to the child, now grown up, leaving home and going out into the world. There is, of course, an element of sadness in this leaving of home though we may only be moving three miles away. The College has always received so much help, guidance and strength from the Hospital. It is certain that the College will develop its own strong character, and it is time that it should now have its independent existence and fulfil its destiny at Froyle, fighting its own battles ...
>
> We feel we are founding, or rather refounding, something which will exist for all time. We are anxious to make the new College a model for similar enterprises; and this will mean not only establishing its essential services but adding to the facilities which the present College offers. At present the Hospital kitchen supplies all College meals. Hot water, central heating and electric light and power are also provided by the Hospital; even some of the clerical work of the College is undertaken

55   *One of the old wooden buildings shortly before demolition.*

by the Hospital. Since 'the appointed day' these services have been paid for at an agreed rate. At Froyle they will no longer be available, and the College will indeed have to fend for itself.

In November, the new Warden reported to the Trustees as to how he saw the College developing. He thought there was only a fair chance of increasing the number of boys so long as the College had the existing age limits (15 to 18) and so few training courses. No more than 55 could be accommodated at Froyle without adding to the buildings and there was not room for the staff required. It was suggested that the next stage of building should start as soon as the aim and policy for the future was decided. They should then 'sell the going concern to the Education Authorities as the answer to their prayers.' The Warden thought that the minimum age for admission was too high and that not enough time was given to the general education of the boys. He was convinced that they must provide new training courses that would lead to employment in offices rather than workshops so that they could attract boys of 'reasonably high intelligence'. He therefore proposed that the College would provide a good general education for boys aged 11 to 16 with a more advanced one for those aged 16 to 19, if they had the necessary ability and ambition, or specialised technical courses, with some class-work, for those who wanted a specifically vocational training.

Mr Heywood put forward ideas for additional courses—draughtsmanship (especially mechanical drawing), engraving, clerical (shorthand, typing and book-keeping) and poultry and pig keeping. The Warden's proposals on age and courses were adopted.

In the spring of 1953 Miss Treloar wa invited to plant a tulip tree and a catalpa in the open ground between the new buildings and the garages. The site was now ready for occupation and the move was carried out during the Easter holidays. On 27 April 1953 the College started its new life, leaving behind the battered old wooden buildings that had been its home for nearly 45 years. Sadly, Miss Treloar did not live to see the move, having died a short while before.

Eighteen months after the move, the Trustees made a contribution towards the memorial to Miss Florence Treloar that the Hospital Management Committee had organised. It was also decided to have a copy made of the bust of Sir William Treloar that was at the Hospital and place it on the north face of the south wing of the new buildings at Froyle.

56   *The new workshops.*

57   *The trees planted by Miss Treloar can just be seen in the lawn.*

9

Froyle — Lord Mayor Treloar College

The summer term of 1953 began with 44 boys—all that could be accommodated. The Trustees then decided to extend in order to increase the number by another 70 and the plan had the support of the Ministry of Education. The new buildings were to consist of dormitories and common rooms, six classrooms, rooms for two more training courses, a swimming bath and remedial gymnasium. The plans were prepared by Christopher Green, who had also done those for the conversion of Froyle Place. The new boarding house was to be called Burnham House to commemorate Lord Burnham, who was the College's Chairman of Trustees for many years. The accommodation in Froyle Place was known as Jephson House after previous owners of the estate.

Shortly after the move to Froyle, the boys' uniform was changed to a smart, dark green blazer with a small monogram (the letters LMTC arranged horizontally in red and the College crest) on the pocket and grey flannel trousers. The tie was to be green with the letters LMTC arranged vertically in red.

In addition to the technical training, which occupied more than three quarters of the working time, each boy followed a course of general education suited to his aptitude and ability. English, History, Geography, Mathematics and General Knowledge were on the curriculum and Scripture was taught to each class. All boys were given pocket money every week according to their seniority and could get a monthly bonus for 'hard work and progress in their training'.

The boys attended prayers each morning and a College Service on Sunday mornings in Froyle Parish Church. Those who were Catholics could go to the Roman Catholic Church in Alton. The College also enlisted the help of the Youth Employment Officers and the Ministry of Labour to try and find suitable jobs for those about to leave.

In early 1955 an application was made to the Ministry of Education for recognition as a Non-Maintained Special School and this was approved. A month later, the Trustees decided to get information about the fees being charged in schools of a similar nature so that they could apply for approval for a fee in line with that generally operative. By April that year a few boys were starting to take General Certificate of Education (GCE) examinations at

58   *The Main Hall in Froyle Place.*

Ordinary Level (O Levels). Although they had only just settled into their new home, the boys were playing football with matches against local teams, table tennis and going to Farnham Baths to swim. They put on a Christmas Concert and a music prize was established. Several boys were taking music lessons. In their spare time the boys watched films and television and made use of the library.

In July 1956, the Warden reported:

> the new building is now almost complete, and next term, September, 1956, we embark on the great venture of adding a proper school to the

59   *A dormitory in Jephson House.*

present system of training older boys in trades. This means that there will be provision for the full-time general education of physically handicapped boys from the age of 11 to 16, and training courses for boys of 16 and over. A well-qualified teaching staff has been appointed and an instructor for the new training course in shorthand, typing and book-keeping. The teaching staff will number eight and include specialists in History, Geography, French, Mathematics, Science, Art and Handicrafts. A Science Laboratory and an Art and Handicrafts room have been added. The new Remedial Gymnasium with its covered Swimming Pool will be in the charge of a specialist in Physical Education. The Handicraft Room will provide a much greater range of occupational therapy than has been possible as yet, as well as useful and happy employment of free time; and the Swimming Pool will be an invaluable asset towards the physical development and well-being of the boys. There will be a Matron and a Housemaster resident in each building, the old and the new. Present entries show that by September we shall have an encouraging number of new boys for the educational course; all vacancies for training courses are already filled for this year. It is of interest that next term we shall have three boys who will be paid for directly by their parents.

  It was also announced that boys had gained passes in City and Guilds Radio Service Work Examinations and O Levels in English Language and English Literature. The aim was to educate the boys as well as train them to achieve 'a large measure of independence … The College hopes to give them the means of attaining a balanced outlook.' Froyle took its first school pupils in September 1956.

60 *Burnham House and the bust of Sir William Treloar.*

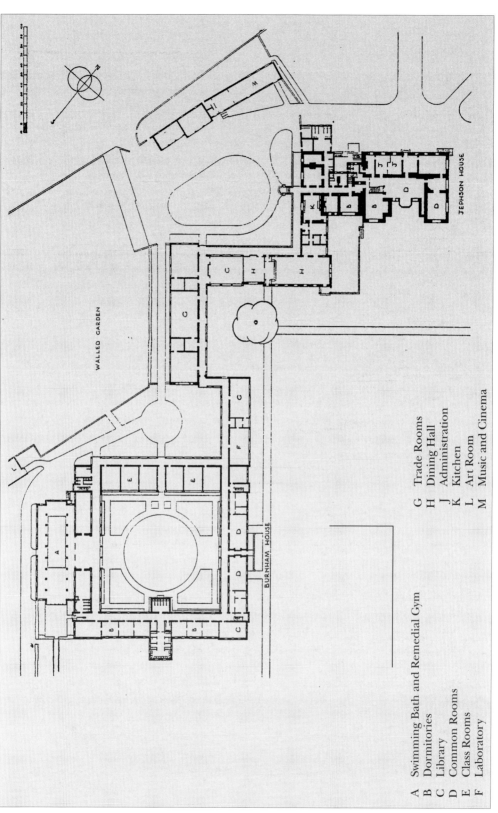

WALLED GARDEN

BURNHAM HOUSE

JEPHSON HOUSE

A Swimming Bath and Remedial Gym
B Dormitories
C Library
D Common Rooms
E Class Rooms
F Laboratory

G Trade Rooms
H Dining Hall
J Administration
K Kitchen
L Art Room
M Music and Cinema

61   *Plan taken from the booklet prepared for the Opening Ceremony of the Completed College, 26 June 1857*

10

Froyle — the Lord Mayor Treloar School and College

The new buildings, built round a courtyard, were opened by Lord Hailsham, Minister of Education, on 26 July 1957. Two educational courses for those aged between 11 and 16 had been started—one was equivalent to a Grammar School course and led to O Levels, while the other was like a Secondary Modern School course and included technical lessons.

1958 was the Golden Jubilee of the College's first opening. The Annual Report for that year showed that at the start of the summer term there were 130 boys—the intended number—with a waiting list for admission. They came from more than 50 education authorities in 34 counties; 62 of the boys lived in Jephson House and 68 in Burnham House, with 53 of them on training courses and the rest in full-time education. The Warden ended by saying:

> it can truthfully be said, we believe, that the College is able to meet the needs of a considerable number of the boys more fully than would be possible anywhere else, for no other establishment exists which is able to the same extent to cater both for severe physical disability and high intellectual ability, without excluding the less physically handicapped or the less intellectually gifted. We hope it is not extravagant to say what, indeed, many of us who work in the College feel; that if ever money has been invested in human welfare and happiness, it has been in Sir William Treloar's foundation, now 50 years old.

In December of that year, the first group of full-time GCE candidates faced the examiners. The nine boys who were entered passed 47 out of a possible 62 subjects. One boy had eight passes in the following July examination and some of the boys on the training courses had also taken O Levels. Of this first group of pupils from the School, some went on to university with two boys accepted at Oxford in 1963.

As well as studying, the boys took part in cricket, football, water polo, table-tennis and chess matches, playing other schools and local youth clubs. The College had its own magazine, the *Treloar Observer*, which was edited and produced by the boys, as well as two Scout troops—one in each House. Other activities

62   *Lord Hailsham signing autographs.*

63   *Out-of-school activities.*

64   *The Science laboratory.*

65   *A common room.*

66   *A school classroom.*

included swimming, archery and art, a Model Railway Club, Stamp Club, Film Society, Natural History Society, Photographic Society, Air Rifle Club, Choir and a Bible Fellowship. In the winter there were gramophone concerts and a College entertainment was performed at the end of the Christmas term.

All of these out-of-school activities caused the Warden to ask the Trustees to consider providing a building to house them. The Chairman suggested that a new assembly hall might be built and then the present one could be adapted for recreational purposes. By January 1961 it had been decided to ask for an estimate for a hall to seat 130-50 people plus 50 wheelchairs, with a stage and rooms at the back. As it happened, the new assembly hall had to wait for several years while the Trustees concentrated on building a boarding school for physically handicapped girls. Known as the Florence Treloar School for Girls, its story is told later.

By 1961 boys in all four of the indoor training courses took external examinations. More of the younger boys were taking O Levels and some had gone on to grammar schools in order to prepare for Advanced Level (A Level). In September of that year, to the delight of the boys, a rally of vintage Rolls-Royces was held at the College and about 30 cars attended.

The College was subjected to a Ministry of Education inspection for four days in June 1963. The report said that 'the Warden has evolved an effective, neat and tidy organisation in all departments. It now remains to provide greater flexibility to allow for the varying needs of individual boys, and to work towards the full development and extension of the academic courses.' It was suggested that there should be more use of individual physiotherapy as well as psychological and psychiatric services—several boys had been asked to leave on account of behaviour problems. More house tutors and 'house mothers' were needed and much of the equipment was not geared to handicapped boys. The medical conditions were noted and the biggest groups were those who had had poliomyelitis, haemophiliacs and those with cerebral palsy. They made up almost two thirds of the boys. The report continued with comments that were to be made on and off for the next 40 years:

> as the site is very exposed, glazing or wind breaks at strategic points where boys congregate in the open cloisters would be very welcome in wet, windy, or wintry weather …. Burnham House has rather a bleak and unhomely atmosphere … the main sick bay … is inconveniently sited as it is a long way from the kitchen … some smaller rooms need to be made available for the teaching of small groups.

A month after the inspection, the College had a more welcome visitor. Queen Frederika of Greece arrived on the morning of 11 July and went on a tour, seeing the houses, dining room, training courses, gymnasium, swimming pool, classrooms and sick bay. The same year, the College was adopted by *Canberra*, the flagship of the P & O fleet. Members of the crew came to the College and the boys were invited to visit the ship.

In September 1963, the Trustees began to discuss their 10-year Development Plan. This was to include the building of an assembly hall with a 'Music School'. The area being used for assemblies would then become a hobbies room, lecture room for instructors and Jephson House games room. The Commercial Studies class could then

67 *Visit of Queen Frederika of Greece, 11 July 1963.*

68   *View of the College before the assembly hall was built.*

go into the existing Jephson House games room. There was also to be a library (with cycle sheds behind), medical unit and gymnasium with room for indoor archery. In the future, it was planned to develop some residential sheltered industry for ex-students.

In order to raise the money for the Development Plan, a national appeal was launched and the Trust film, 'There's no Discouragement', was shown to audiences throughout the country. Apart from the development of the Boys' College, it was hoped to fund up to 12 Commonwealth Scholarships and a sheltered residence and employment centre for 60 handicapped men and women.

In March 1965 the Trustees met with the Department of Education and Science to discuss the plans for the new 'Cultural Centre'. This was now to be anassembly hall with a stage, two dressing rooms and toilets, a music room and music practice rooms, a library and muniments room, craft, art and pottery classrooms, an exhibition foyer, as well as an office and technical library. A medical unit and sick bay had also been designed as part of the complex. The Department commented that they had 'looked at the plans which will provide very grandiose and lavish provision,' but added, 'we will be interested in the effect on running costs.' They pointed out that the buildings would have a long life and that 'there may be a great many changes even during so short a period as the next 20 years not only possibly in teaching methods but in the development of subjects both during school hours and afterwards.' The Department thought that the music, stage and arts areas should be on the same level, that the library might prove too small (they suggested enlarging it by making the dressing rooms double as music practice rooms) and that the design of the female toilets should take into account the fact that disabled girls from Florence Treloar's might use them. Following this, the architects increased the library size by 30 per cent, improved the female toilet facilities and replanned the art block. It was hoped to have this phase finished by the end of 1968—the Diamond Jubilee Year.

While all this planning was taking place, there were other developments. The Warden engaged a part-time physiotherapist for three sessions a week, Air-Rifle and Sailing Clubs were formed and the colour film of the College gained a gold medal at the 2nd International Film Festival on Rehabilitation of the Disabled in Rome. In 1964 it was decided to buy a school bus, with half of the cost being donated by the Variety Club of Great Britain, and Alyn Wilde, the art master, was asked to copy the portrait of Miss Florence Treloar that hung in the Hospital. He was to paint several portraits of staff and Trustees over the years.

In January 1965 news came that one old boy had been awarded an open exhibition at Downing College, Cambridge, whilst another had an open scholarship to Magdalen College, Oxford. The Lord Mayor of London visited the College at Froyle and the new Girls' School at Holybourne in July that year. Such visits had been an annual event before the separation of the Hospital and College but had not taken place since then. The Lord Mayor had been due to come in May but the date was changed due to the opening of the Kennedy Memorial at Runnymede.

Early in 1967 the Department of Education was sent the plans for Phase II of the Development Plan. This consisted of building a medical wing with two seven-bed wards, an isolation ward, day room, etc., reconstructing Burnham House (to become Burnham East and Burnham West) and modifiying and extending the existing gymnasium.

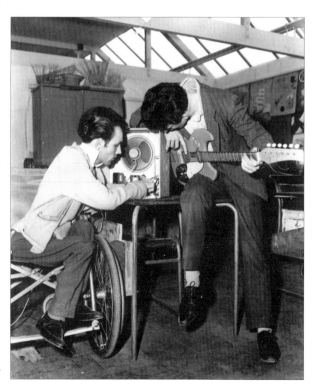

69 *Music practice!*

70   *Pen and ink design by Seamus Whelan and Mr A. Wilde.*

The archery/rifle range was not now included. The Burnham House conversion was to include a tuck shop, Housemaster's office, games room, and photographic and dark rooms on the ground floor with the dormitories and staff accommodation on the first floor. It was estimated that the Medical Wing would cost £50,000, the Burnham work £2,500 and the gymnasium alterations £10,500. Priority was to be given to the first two projects. The Department of Education approved the plans for this phase subject to two small alterations.

In February 1967 there had been another Inspection. The report noted that 'the classrooms and workshops are widely spaced out along long, cold, open corridors', although the original mansion, in which the seniors lived, did 'help to convey an atmosphere of home'. The Inspector 'thought the boys friendly and welcoming, but more resigned rather than forward looking. They are treated warmly as individuals, and have a welcome degree of freedom in ordering their lives. But they are rather bored, especially at weekends.' It was suggested that there be 'joint VI form work with the new Girls' School.' On a later visit, it was thought that 'there is a sturdy and cheerful independence about the boys, and they have the ability to stand back and take a good humoured look at themselves.'

Perhaps as a response to the complaints of boredom, golf instruction was started at the College, with the Golf Foundation paying the professional's fees and the cost of equipment. More archery equipment was purchased as well as a 'training motor car'. One of the training courses ceased when it was decided to close down the pig and poultry unit as there was little interest in it.

During the autumn term of 1967 the rooms in the assembly hall block were brought into use. This was followed by all the other alterations that were part of Phase I of the Development Plan.

The 1968 Annual Report showed that, as earlier in Treloar's history, the disabilities suffered by the pupils were changing. The most common ones now were poliomyelitis, cerebral palsy, muscular dystrophy, spina bifida, brittle bones, rheumatic conditions and haemophilia. There were 39 haemophiliacs at the College and a grant had been awarded to the College for research into methods of treatment of the condition, in close co-operation with the Oxford Haemophilia Centre. Dr S.G. Rainsford was appointed as a Research Fellow in October 1968, establishing a research laboratory at Lord Mayor Treloar Hospital.

In the same month, alterations were made to the College's rules. Up until this time, all public houses had been out of bounds to all the boys. Now, those over 18 were allowed in a pub unless they were found there with a boy under 18—in which case they would lose the privilege for at least a term. Boys were not allowed to loiter at or outside any of the College gates and, unless they had a special exemption, boys were to do such domestic work as their Housemasters directed. All boys under 18 had to wear the College blazer and tie when visiting Alton or other towns. Playing cards could be used only according to Housemaster's rules.

Boys had to get up at 7.00 a.m. and then make their beds and do domestic work. This was followed by roll-call and inspection. Breakfast was at 8.05 a.m. and assembly at 9.00 a.m. There were four lessons in the morning with a break of 15 minutes. Afternoon work started at 2.10 p.m. with tea at 3.45 p.m. Between 4.00 and 5.00 p.m., the boys were at prep or in the workshops and supper was at 7.30 p.m. The boys in the Junior Houses had to be in their

71   *The Tailor's shop.*

72   *The visit of Princess Alexandra, 5 February 1969.*

dormitories by 8.00 p.m. This was followed by a roll-call by dormitory, silence
for prayers and lights out. The Senior House had lights out at 9.30 p.m.

The highlight of the Diamond Jubilee year was the visit, on 5 February 1969,
of HRH Princess Alexandra to open the new buildings at the College, including
the assembly hall, named the Newton-Davis Hall after Colonel Charles Newton-
Davis, a Trustee and then Chairman between 1950 and 1966.

In July 1969 the Warden retired, to be replaced by the first Headmaster of
the College, Peter Johnston-Smith. He came from Worksop College where
he had been Housemaster and Head of History. Mr Johnston-Smith began
to make changes within weeks of starting. In October 1969 he approached
the Trustees, who agreed in principle 'that the College should participate in
computer education to enable pupils to receive basic tuition in this subject.'
It was later decided to approach ICL with a view to their helping with the cost,
and they agreed to a 10 per cent discount.

In the *Treloar Observer* of Christmas 1969, the new Headmaster wrote about
his first impressions of the College. He hoped that 'the new Advisory Committee drawn from the boys of all the Houses will show itself to be activeminded
and responsible.' He believed 'that education is not just something that goes
on in schools and colleges; education is part of life, and life is not just con-
fined to term time.' Because of this, he wanted the staff to meet and get to
know the boys' parents. In order to make it easier for the boys to get out to
Alton, the Headmaster asked for there to be more transport provided on Saturdays so that the boys would not have to get lifts from the public.

73   *The Radio and TV Servicing workshop.*

74   *The Commercial Studies course.*

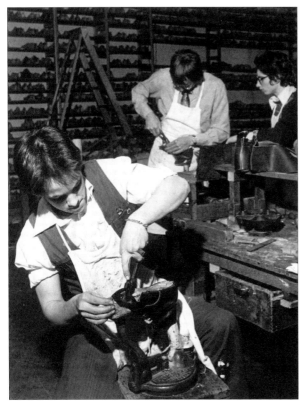

75   *The Boot and Shoe shop.*

With the arrival of the Headmaster came closer links with Florence Treloar School at Holybourne. In February 1970 the Headmaster and Headmistress put forward some joint proposals—they had become convinced that 'coeducation is not only feasible but desirable'. They thought that this would make better use of resources and avoid 'duplication in teaching, welfare, maintenance and administration'. They suggested a two-form entry, co-educational 'middle' school at Holybourne for those between nine and 12 years old, and a two-form co-educational senior school at Froyle with an age range from 12 to 18/19 years. They hoped this could happen from September 1974. They were also of the opinion that the training courses should change 'in order to integrate them into the school curriculum, e.g. CSE (Certificate of Secondary Education), O Level or A Level based courses such as Metalwork, Engineering, Commerce, Principle of Accounts, Home Economics, Handcraft, etc., instead of the present "City & Guilds" based courses'. When co-education eventually became a reality in 1978, the Senior School was, in fact, located at Holybourne in order to be nearer to Alton.

The Headmaster also concerned himself with more day-to-day matters—a telephone call box was installed in Burnham House, an 11 Plus Class Dinghy was bought for the Sailing Club and Mr Gasston was given permission to buy three television sets from the tuck shop profits. Later that year, it was also agreed to install a hot-drinks vending machine, and a French exchange was arranged for the following summer.

By September 1970 the curriculum had been reorganised so that boys on the Training Courses could take school subjects as needed rather than follow a set pattern of traditional teaching.

In early 1971 plans were put forward for a 'Hostel type building for the use of the more senior boys of the College'. This was to be built on the western side of the 'Hen and Chicken Hill', on the area now providing extra staff car parking. There were to be single and double study bedrooms for 15 boys as well as a lounge, TV and games area and a sun terrace. Thought was also given to the possibility of converting the Oast House into a hostel. Town planning approval was obtained for the former plan, but it was decided to shelve the idea in December as the numbers of pupils were not forthcoming. This did not deter the improving links between College and School though; the *Treloar Observer* of Easter 1971 described a social at the School to which some of the boys had been invited. The theme of the evening was 'Make Love, Not War!' and the event seems to have been a success!

During the early 1970s came the first application for a child suffering from the consequences of the drug Thalidomide and, about the same time, the Trustees agreed to accept students with controlled epilepsy. These and other changes caused staffing problems in the houses as an increasing number of boys were needing more assistance with dressing and personal care. Night staff were also employed as a temporary measure whilst an alarm system was investigated. In March 1973 it was agreed that the provision of a Hydrotherapy Pool and Physiotherapy Centre was important for the many boys suffering from haemophilia.

76   *A Tailoring class.*

More changes in teaching at the College came when the Headmaster decided that class teaching should give way to group and individual teaching. He thought this was especially important in French, P.E. and English.

The Trustees also made changes. They decided that in order to have closer contact with staff at the School and College, up to six members of the teaching, nursing, appeals and administrative staff should be invited to a buffet lunch after the monthly Trustee meetings. Trustee Lt General Sir William Pike was appointed to be Governor for Staff Liaison for the College and Mrs Bootle-Wilbraham for the School.

All through the early 1970s, a Working Party was looking into future Trust policy. In 1973 they reported that a co-educational Sixth Form should be formed, co-operating with local schools and sixth form colleges. They hoped that girls could be encouraged to join some of the vocational courses at the College and that a Junior Form of boys and girls aged nine to 11 should be introduced at the School.

As far as the boys were concerned, there were more pressing matters. In the summer of 1973, they petitioned for the rules regarding the length of hair to be relaxed. The Headmaster told the Trustees 'that as two female hairdressers were now employed, the matter might well resolve itself.'

The summer of 1974 saw the retirement of Mr Johnston-Smith and he was replaced by Alec Macpherson. The new Headmaster introduced trophies for badminton, basketball, table tennis, snooker and athletics. Genetic counselling began and the Houses were rearranged, with Burnham West taking the younger boys, who then moved to Burnham East and then on to Jephson. The Headmaster asked for guards to be put over all the radiators and for hoists to be provided in the houses. He then set about arranging some more practical but non-vocational CSE and non-examination courses. From this time, all First Form boys and those who had difficulty with writing were taught typing and the green blazers were to be gradually phased out and replaced by navy blue ones.

Changes for the staff were also discussed. The Headmaster suggested that the retirement age for new staff should be 60 and the Trustees investigated the possibility of building some two-bedroomed bungalows for retired employees.

In order to generate more income, the Trust wondered if the vocational courses could be opened to the able-bodied. The Trust solicitor could see no problems as long as those doing the courses paid and the money was used to provide better facilities for the boys.

In spring 1975 a full-time occupational therapist was appointed to work at both the College and School, advising on electronic aids, special equipment and furniture. A remedial gymnast and hydrotherapist also started at the College and Mr Maitland became Deputy Headmaster. Twenty boys began to work for the Duke of Edinburgh Award and, as some of them wished to include animal husbandry in their course, a local farmer supplied some pigs to live in the sties on the former College Farm during term time. By October 1975 32 boys were working towards the Bronze award and five towards the Silver.

The mid-1970s were worrying times for the Trust. Mrs Warnock had visited the School and College in July 1974 while gathering information for her Report, and it was feared that this could greatly affect the future of Treloar's. There were cuts in local expenditure on education, the birth rate was falling, the Government's policy was to integrate handicapped children into state schools and, due to medical advances, the number of pupils with spina bifida and haemophilia would fall. It was also recognised that the accommodation at both School and College was below what was now expected, especially for the older students. Other similar colleges were offering more comfort, privacy and amenities. Several possible future options were considered, including, if numbers of pupils dropped dramatically, the closure of the College, sale of all the Froyle properties, and building on the field to the north of the School in Holybourne. Training courses could then be based at the new Alton Sixth Form College and outlying technical colleges.

78 *The Electronics course.*

79 *A visit from R.A.F. Odiham.*

The new Trust Chairman, Lt General Sir William Pike, organised meetings with local education authorities, at which it was agreed that there needed to be more emphasis on remedial education for the younger pupils. For those aged 16 and over, it was thought that their courses 'should educate for living i.e. self-independence preferably within a self contained flat learning cooking, etc.' There was a worry that students could leave at 18 unable to cope with the outside world. The authorities said that they would prefer them to 'spend an extra two years in school and take the examinations over an extended period.' Everyone was in favour of co-education and thought that the Senior School should be at Holybourne and the Junior School at Froyle. Sir William then went to speak to the staff at the School and College and listen to their views and suggestions.

Having decided to merge the School and College, the Trust offered the post of Principal of the amalgamated schools to Mr Macpherson on 21 March 1977. At the same time, Miss Anderson (Head of Florence Treloar School) was offered that of Vice Principal and Head of the Senior School. Both offers were accepted and the staff were told of the appointments the same afternoon. It was decided to call the new establishment 'Lord Mayor Treloar College' and the individual premises 'Upper School' (at Holybourne) and 'Lower School' (at Froyle). The Haemophilia Unit was to be sited at Holybourne instead of Froyle, with the younger boys being transported there when they needed to attend. Plans then began in earnest to try to have the alterations ready by September 1978.

By October things were not going so well. The proposed daily programme for the new College had caused distress among the Florence Treloar School staff. They were not happy with the possible length of the school day or school year, the disregard of their existing contracts and the plans for Saturday mornings.

The autumn of 1977 saw the formation of the League of Friends to the Treloar Trust Schools. Over 100 local residents joined and many volunteered to help on shopping expeditions, assist staff on outings and support in other ways.

While all the planning and discussion went on among the staff, life went on as usual for the boys. Patrick Moore gave a talk on astronomy, and Jim Fox, the 1976 Olympic Pentathlon Gold Medal winner, spent a day at the College. There were trips to France and Germany and five boys gained their silver Duke of Edinburgh Awards. A new coach was donated and used for visits such as those to HMS *Victory*, the Tower of London and the Queen's Review of the Fleet. College boys took part in the Southern Area Games and Stoke Mandeville Junior Games, gaining many medals. Several pupils were awarded their Royal Yachting Association Elementary Sailing Certificates and the boys on the Electronics course designed and made two audio compasses for blind sailors.

80   *College boys sailing.*

11

HOLYBOURNE — THE FLORENCE TRELOAR SCHOOL

As far back as 1909 Sir William Treloar had hoped to be able to receive crippled girls for industrial training, but a lack of funds had prevented it. The subject was considered again in 1927 when the Trustees discussed the extension of the College to include the training of girls, and in 1946, when it was agreed to rebuild the College, the plan was to accommodate both disabled boys and girls. None of these plans ever came to fruition.

At last, in the 1958 Jubilee Appeal, the Chairman, Lord Burnham, reported that 'on the invitation of the Ministry of Education it is hoped to add to the present foundation a similar college for girls.' In July that year the Trustees debated whether the proposed establishment for girls should provide general education only, training only or, as at the boys' College, education and training. It was also decided that they could not 'consider the erection of an Institution remote from the present College'. Despite this, in October 1959 the Bursar was asked to see if there were any possible properties for sale in a radius of 20 miles. One of the reasons was that this would give 'suitable surroundings immediately, without having to wait for gardens to be developed, trees to grow, etc.' Grayshott Hall and Langley Court, near Liss, were investigated but not thought to be suitable, and so in early 1960 architect Mr Alwyn was asked to 'ascertain which site, in his opinion, would be the most suitable from the point of levels, etc.' in fields owned by the Trust lying on the west of Howards Lane, Holybourne. Part of the Froyle Place Estate was to be sold to finance the venture.

By July 1960 outline planning permission had been obtained and detailed plans began to be drawn up. Visits were made to various other schools for handicapped children, and landscape architects were consulted. On 12 October 1961 the Trustees met with the Ministry of Education, who suggested planning for 50-60 girls, but the Trust decided that the School should be for 100 'able and gifted physically handicapped girls'.

After seeing the plans, the Ministry thought that 'the teaching and therapy area should be closely linked to the dining area and to the recreational spaces, and that the two latter zones should have a close affinity with the sleeping area,' and they made several practical suggestions for improvements to the plans. The Trustees were concerned about spending too much of their capital on the proposed girls' school, as that would reduce their income from the remaining capital with which they subsidised the fees charged for the College. There was also a new Burnham salary award for teachers to be taken into account.

The target date for completion of the girls' school was March 1965, which would enable it to open for the start of the summer term. Formal approval from the Minister of Education had to be obtained, a footpath diverted and overhead electricity cables removed before building could start. The estimated cost for the whole project was £333,000, excluding equipment (the final cost came to just over £480,000). Priority was given to the building of houses for the Headmistress and Head Gardener, and work started on 7 August 1962.

The Trustees decided to appoint a Headmistress well in advance of the opening date so that she could be involved in the planning and the choice of furniture and equipment, and in October 1962 the advert was published. The Ministry described it as a 'unique and very interesting appointment'. Miss A.A.M. Wells, Headmistress of Shrewsbury High School, was appointed to start on 1 September 1963.

81   *The site of Florence Treloar School showing the overhead electricity cables that had to be moved.*

82   *The laying of the foundation stone, 17 May 1963. From left to right: Colonel Newton-Davis (chairman), Mr Alwyn (architect), Mr Cannon (builder), Hon. Mrs Gilmor (Trustee) and the clerk of works.*

83   *Miss Wells inspecting the new buildings.*

Building work progressed and on 17 May 1963 the Chairman of the Trustees, Lt Col C. Newton-Davis, laid the foundation stone. Miss Barlee was appointed Senior Mistress, and by September 1964 10 applications for entry had already been received. A two-day conference for all the teaching staff who were to take up their duties in September was held at the end of April 1965.

The Ministry of Education made a visit in May 1965 in order to check on progress. The report noted that the premises appeared to be completed together with decorations and fixtures and that all was tasteful and well furnished. Equipment had been ordered and tarmac drives had been laid with small trees planted near the boundary. The Ministry's conclusion was that it 'should be a delightful school to work in when equipped.' Apart from the Headmistress and Senior Mistress, seven other teaching staff had been appointed as well as a Matron and Assistant Matron.

The Times Educational Supplement of 25 June 1965 reported that 'The Florence Treloar School, a new grammar school for physically handicapped girls, will receive its first pupils on September 24.' The day before the opening, the *Daily Telegraph* ran an article entitled 'Crippled Girls' Own Boarding School'. The new pupils were aged from 10 to 18 and they came from 18 different counties. The fees were £678 a year for boarders. A fifth of the girls had suffered from polio, and other disabilities included spina bifida, cerebral palsy and brittle bones.

The new School received several gifts, including a donation from SS *Iberia* (which adopted the School), which was used to buy canoes. The Variety Club of Great Britain had a coach made and delivered, and its first outing was to Stoke Mandeville. The first 'expedition' abroad was to Holland in 1967.

In April 1966 an Inspector visited the School. He noted that a five-year course was already established, with one girl taking A Levels that year. 'The school seems to have started well, but there are a number of points of organisation, etc., on which H.M. [Headmistress] will want to have second thoughts.' Ten months later, there was another visit. This time it was thought:

> the selection procedure is odd, and inadequate … The prevailing impression is, however, one of a rather dour, uncompromising determination to pretend that all these girls are able to follow a "normal" academic education; much of the teaching is academic cramming, with little understanding of the problems or of the specific needs of handicapped girls.

The report continued, 'the buildings are vast, with corridors of unbelievable length … The classrooms are bare and uninteresting. The swimming pool is badly planned.'

Despite these depressing comments, the girls had lots of out-of-class interests. Musical options included learning the piano, clarinet, violin or recorder, while archery and riding were available and swimming proved very popular, with many girls gaining ASA awards. A Guide Company was formed as well as a Sixth Form Society.

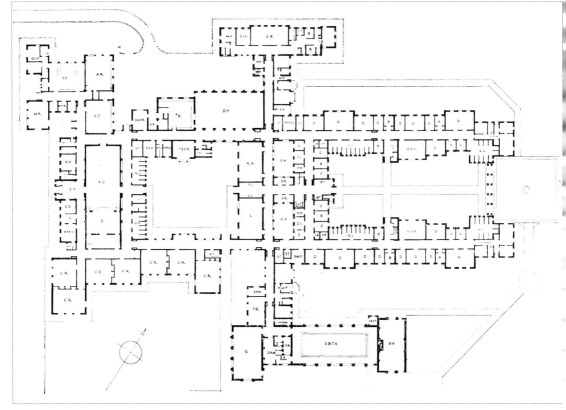

84   *Plan of Florence Treloar School*

AH	Assembly Hall	HW	Hair Washing
AHMF	Assistant House Mistress' Flats	IB	Isolation Block
AR	Art Room	K	Kitchen
B	Bathroom	KSRR	Kitchen Staff Rest Room
BO	Bursar's Office	L	Library
BH	Boiler House	LN	Linen
BT	Boots	LT	Lift
C	Cleaners	MAO	Matron's Office
CL	Cloaks	MF	Matron's Flat
CR	Classrooms	ML	Men's Laboratory
D	Dormitories	MO	Medical Officer
DH	Dining Hall	MPR	Music Practice Room
DR	Drying Rooms	MR	Music Room
DS	Domestic Science	NN	Night Nurse
DSDR	Domestic Staff Dining Room	OA	Open Areas
DSIF	Domestic Science Instruction Flat	PG	Playground
DSL	Domestic Staff Lavatories	RR	Recreation Room
DSO	Domestic Superintendent's Office	S	Stage
DYR	Day Room	SB	Sick Bay
E	Enquiries	SBFP	Swimming Bath Filtration Plant
EH	Entrance Hall	SBTH	Swimming Bath
FA	First Aid	SH	Showers
G	Gymnasium	SL	Small Laundries
GL	Girls' Lavatories	SO	Secretary's Office
GS	General Science Laboratory	SPH	Speech Therapy
GSR	Girls' Sitting Rooms	ST	Stores
HMF	House Mistress' Flat	TR	Therapy
HMO	House Mistress' Office	TSDR	Teaching Staff Dining Room
HMS	Headmistress' Study	TSL	Teaching Staff Lavatories

85 *Princess Alexandra unveiling the portrait of Miss Florence Treloar, 2 May 1967.*

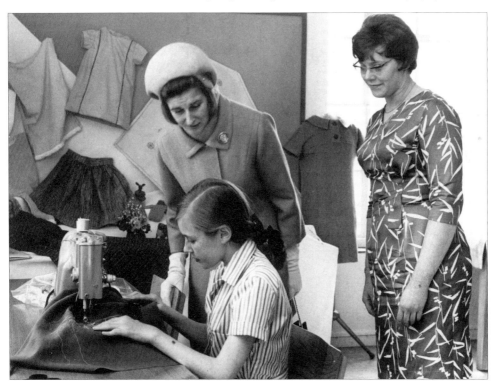

86 *Princess Alexandra on her tour of the School.*

87   *A cookery class.*

88   *The School and College teams from the Junior Paraplegic Games held at Stoke Mandeville, 1971.*

On 2 May 1967 Princess Alexandra performed the official opening of the Florence Treloar School. After lunch at the College and being welcomed at the School by Mr Stanley Evans, Chairman of the Trustees, the Princess unveiled a portrait of Miss Florence Treloar painted by Alyn Wilde of the College. She then went on a tour of the School. A report of the visit, written some time later by a pupil, recalled the staff practising curtsies beforehand, Princess Alexandra's turquoise blue coat and daffodil yellow hat, the Army playing 'Puppet on a String' and the scarlet helicopter.

By the autumn term of 1967, the number had risen to 83 girls. During that term the pupils were involved in all kinds of events. At Holybourne there was a demonstration by Yardley, the cosmetic firm, a sale in aid of Save the Children and an entertainment at Christmas. Girls went out to a Careers Conference in Alton, the National Gallery, a school trip to Longleat House and a party at Lord Wandsworth College. During the next year outings included visiting the Russian Orthodox Church in London, the Junior Sports at Stoke Mandeville, Covent Garden Theatre, the Ideal Homes' Exhibition, Wimbledon and a sailing weekend at Calshot.

The Headmistress, Miss Wells, was awarded the 1969 Churchill Travelling Fellowship to enable her to travel in America and Canada investigating education there for the physically handicapped and Miss Barlee was appointed Acting Head. On her return to the School, Miss Wells began to work with the new Headmaster at the College to explore ways of bringing the two establishments closer together with the ultimate aim of co-education.

Four years after the opening of the School, the girls published the first issue of volume 1 of their magazine, *Enterprise*. In it were a list of the examination successes in A Level and O Level, news of Old Girls, reports of sporting activities such as water polo, canoeing, horse riding and a Sixth Form camp, as well as poems and articles by pupils. May 1970 saw the first Old Girls' Reunion take place and it was then decided to form an official Old Girls' Association.

89   *The unveiling of the portrait of Miss Wells, 1973. From left to right: Miss Anderson (Head-mistress), Miss Wells (Headmistress 1965-71), Mr Evans (Chairman) and Mrs Bootle-Wilbraham (Trustee).*

A later edition of the School Magazine included an article on 'The Joys of having a "Noddy" Car'. It seems that after four driving lessons in a motorised invalid carriage (known as a 'Noddy' car) and then a solo drive, you were trusted to go out alone, having first stated clearly where and when you are going, if you were 'good enough'. The vehicles did about 40 miles to the gallon and had no room for passengers.

In June 1970 Miss Wells announced her intention of retiring at the end of the summer term 1971. The post was advertised and Miss Anderson was selected to succeed. When she left, Miss Wells wrote, 'I am grateful for having had the opportunity to be in on "the ground floor" of the Florence Treloar School.'

1971 was a particularly good year for sport at the School and College. Teams from both establishments went to the Junior Multi-disabled Games at Stoke Mandeville and came back with many awards including the team trophy. Jenny Orpwood won every field and track event she entered and, on 20 June, three of the girls were at Stoke Mandeville for the British National Games. Two of them, Pauline Dukelow and Jenny Orpwood, were chosen to go to the Paralympic Games at Heidelberg. Both girls were then invited to represent their country in the Commonwealth Paraplegic Games in New Zealand. While there, Jenny won seven medals and former pupil Denise Smith also won the same number in the swimming and track events. Both girls were given financial help by several local Alton organisations.

The early 1970s saw at least one pupil going to Eggar's Grammar School in Alton for classes in subjects not offered by the School. In order to get to the classroom there for A Level French, Lucy Savage had to be carried up two flights of stairs and 'was quite convinced that my end was near'. Extra-curricular activities included pony-trekking in the New Forest, canoeing to the Isle of Wight, visiting France, Belgium, Holland and Germany and winning a debating competition organised by Alton Rotary Club. Dramatic productions included 'Barbarina', 'Trial by Jury' and 'A Midsummer Night's Dream' and there was a variety concert, which was a joint venture with the boys of the College.

After leaving, former pupils went in a great variety of directions. Old Girls were working in banks, offices, a telephone exchange and local government. Those who had just left were studying at training colleges, technical colleges, colleges of art and music or with the Open University.

The new Headmistress, Miss Anderson, was a wheelchair-user herself and became exasperated about the lack of accessibility and car parking for disabled people in Alton. She had 'made fruitless attempts to communicate with Hampshire County Council' and therefore wrote to the local county councillor, suggesting that he accompany girls in wheelchairs to the town to appreciate the difficulties they experienced. A month later, the local police promised to raise the matter with Hampshire Constabulary and the county council promised to lower the kerb stones within 18 months! The Headmistress had an article on the problem published in the journal *Social Services*.

90   *A Science lesson.*

91   *Some of the different equipment used by pupils when typing.*

In 1975 Miss Anderson addressed the Congress of the British Association of
Organisers and Lecturers in Physical Education. As she explained, the School
had been set up as a grammar school but 'by 1970 it was evident that this was
not a true description.' The School, she said, now took girls of average and
above average ability who could benefit from an academic education. There
were 90 pupils with an age range of nine to 19 and about 60 staff, including
15 teachers, 15 nursing and care staff, physiotherapists, office staff, drivers,
gardeners, maintenance men, kitchen and dining room staff and cleaners.
The Sixth Form was quite small, with only 14 girls, six of whom were attending
Eggar's Grammar School.

The Headmistress explained that the range of disabilities had changed
significantly over the 10 years of the School's existence. About three-quarters
of the girls now used a wheelchair, especially for long distances. Ten of the
wheelchairs were electric and the School had hand-propelled go-carts and a
few tricycles. She then went on to describe the working day, which was:

> from 8.50 a.m. to 5.40 p.m. allowing music lessons, physiotherapy, horse
> riding and swimming to be timetabled without usually taking a child
> from other lessons. There is however, a one-and-a-half hour lunch break
> and a half-hour tea break when children can take a well-earned rest or
> get outside.

There was training in self-care, and typing was taught to all First Formers,
with some girls needing electric typewriters. Cookery was taken by all girls
from the Second Form upwards.

In May 1974 the Trustees discussed the effect of the possible reorganisation
of education in Alton. They were prepared to sell a portion of land near the
School to the county as a site for a sixth form college, but this offer was not
taken up.

September 1975 saw the opening of a junior unit at the School, for boys and
girls aged between nine and eleven. Initially there were eight boys and eight
girls. At about this time a group of girls was taken on a field trip to Churchtown
Farm, Cornwall, and a party went to Iceland. In 1976 Susan Sherrell, the Head
Girl, went to the Paralympic Games in Toronto and returned with three gold
medals for swimming.

Behind the scenes, the amalgamation of the School and College was being
discussed and plans were made for the changes to be effected for September
1978. It was decided that Holybourne was to become the site of the Upper
School, giving the older pupils access to the town of Alton. In November 1977
the resignation of Miss Anderson due to ill health was sadly announced, and
Hugh Cocksedge took over as Acting Head of the School.

12

Lord Mayor Treloar College—
Upper and Lower Schools

The Annual Report of the new Lord Mayor Treloar College for 1978-9 announced:

> Thanks to the co-operation of all members of Staff, the amalgamation of our two original schools into one co-educational establishment took place, as planned, at the beginning of the Autumn Term (1978). The boys and girls at both the Lower School at Froyle and the Upper School at Holybourne, settled down quickly to their new surroundings and the everyday routine of school life.

Of the 258 pupils, there were 134 at the Lower School and 124 at the Upper School. Seven students aged over 16 were taking a full-time horticultural course but the radio, TV and electronics, and surgical shoemaking and repairing courses had ceased. An 'Education for Life' course was introduced at the Upper School in order to prepare students to be as independent as possible when they left. It was recognised that there were employment difficulties for all School and College leavers at the time and the idea was to introduce subjects that could become interests after leaving. There were also practical sessions such as car maintenance, electricity and safety in the home and tailoring.

In the Lower School at Froyle, the youngest children were still all together in a special class with their own teacher. Those aged between 11 and 14 were in the First to Third Forms with three or more streams in each year. In certain subjects, the pupils were taught in sets with an average number of 12 in each group. Where pupils had missed education, remedial lessons were given and teaching staff were also timetabled to be in the sick bay in order to fetch work and supervise those in the wards.

All of the houses at Froyle were divided into three or four units, each of which contained about 10 children and was self-contained with its own dormitories, bathrooms and sitting room. Each house had television and recreation rooms as well.

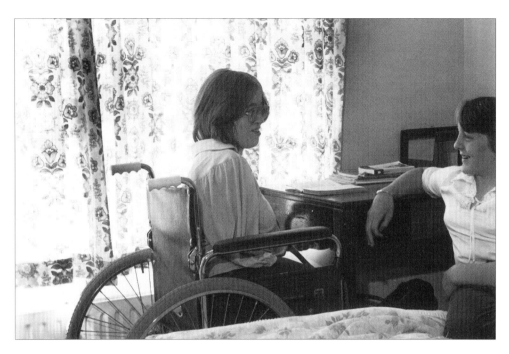

92   *A bedroom in one of the refurbished houses.*

The pupils aged 14 to 20 were based at Holybourne. Those in the Fourth and Fifth Forms (later renumbered Years 10 and 11) had to take English Language, English Literature, Maths, Religious Education, Education for Life, P.E. and Sport. They could then choose four options which might include French, Textiles, Computer Studies, German, Biology, Chemistry and Technical Drawing, amongst other subjects—all of which could be studied as O Levels or CSEs. Time also had to be allowed for other activities such as physiotherapy and Independent Living. At both sites the school day ran from 9.00 a.m. to 4.00 p.m. with preparation periods after tea.

Some of the Sixth Form went to the Alton Sixth Form College for their courses while others stayed at Holybourne to work for RSA and City and Guilds qualifications in commerce, horticulture, tailoring, or took a one-year course with the emphasis on basic English and Maths together with Independence Training and Education for Life. The senior pupils lived in Allan House, which had had a new recreation room built connecting the two blocks. There was also an Independent Living Flat, which most students occupied for a time, doing their own catering and housework.

Parents were given advice on pocket money. It was thought that children in the Junior House would need about 50p a week and the older ones between 50p and £1. Pupils were encouraged to join activities outside Treloar's such as the local Guide Company, Girls' Brigade and to visit local youth clubs. At the Lower School there were sports on Saturday mornings, although parents could collect their children on a Friday evening. Lessons took place on Saturday mornings for those at the Upper School.

After a year, it was found that there was not enough room for all the Sixth Form students in their hostel and so, to make room for them in the other Upper School Houses, 33 of the Fourth Form had to live at Froyle and travel to Holybourne every day for lessons. All the usual outside activities carried on and there were exchange visits, outings and successes in various sporting events. Four girls were presented at Buckingham Palace with their Duke of Edinburgh Gold Awards, the Lower and Upper Schools joined together for the production 'Follow the Star', 11 children went on a pilgrimage to Lourdes and 17 pupils raised over £6,000 for the NSPCC by doing a sponsored canoe paddle on the Basingstoke Canal.

93   *Science in the days before Health and Safety!*

94   *Tailoring at Holybourne.*

95   *Studying for the Business Education Diploma.*

Each year many events would follow the same pattern—the annual visit of the Lord Mayor of London, Old Pupils' Day, Spring and Christmas Fairs, Open Days and Sports Day. There were changes though. In the classroom, 'the range of academic needs has increased and we are helping a large number of children whose progress is held back by all sorts of different learning problems' and so special classes were established for 'slower learners'. In their leisure time, several older students learnt to drive, some pupils spent a week on an Ocean Youth Club cruise, there was success at the Basingstoke Music Festival with the Lower School Choir coming second with Honours, school lunch-time concerts were introduced and hand-bell ringing became popular.

1981 was the International Year of Disabled People. It was appropriate that it was in this year that the number of girls at Treloar's first reached one hundred. The total number of pupils was 264—another record—so it was a good thing that the new kitchens and dining room had just been completed at the Upper School. The Haemophilia Centre moved into new premises there that were paid for by the National Health Service.

As always, many different sports were played during the year, including table tennis, snooker, bowls and archery. A year later, the College wheelchair basketball team was runner-up in the National Championships and one pupil won the Men's Heavyweight Lifting title at the National Senior Paraplegic Games and went on to be selected for the Paralympics.

96   *Hand-bell ringing at an Open Day.*

97   *A game of snooker in the Newton-Davis foyer.*

The highlights of the summer term 1981 were Tom Baker, who played 'Dr Who' in the television series, coming to present prizes and 'Froyle Follies'—an entertainment put on by Lower School pupils and staff. Monday 3 May 1982 was the date of the first sponsored marathon afternoon when nearly £3,000 was raised for the Leprosy Association and the International Boys' Town Trust. The end of that academic year saw the Chairman of the Governing Body, Lt General Sir William Pike, hand over to General Sir David Fraser. Sir William had always shown great personal interest in pupils and staff and was much missed, although he did still continue to visit the Lower School and became Chairman of the League of Friends. His son, Lt Col Hew Pike, Commanding Officer of the 3rd Parachute Regiment, visited the College and recounted his experiences in the recent Falklands Campaign.

An article in the *Hampshire Magazine* of March 1983 gave its readers a glimpse of life at the Lower School. The journalist visited an English class studying the exploits of Theseus and had lunch—'just about the best school meal I have ever had'—in the dining room. At the Upper School she went into one of the houses and saw rooms that showed 'touches of the individual occupants—macho posters, prints of old and young masters, and the occasional cuddly toy.'

The numbers of pupils continued to rise and it was decided that new Sixth Form accommodation was needed. A new building, housing 39 students, two Independent Living Flats and some staff accommodation was built at a cost of £850,000, with £90,000 of that coming from the Department of Education.

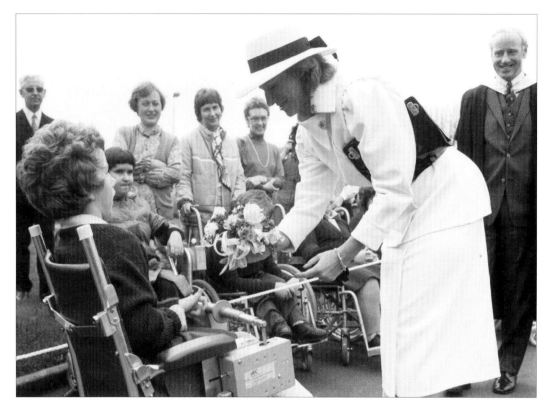

98   *The Duchess of Gloucester being presented with a posy of flowers, 30 October 1984.*

On 30 October 1984 the Duchess of Gloucester came to Holybourne and opened the new building, which was named Gloucester House in honour of her visit. This extra accommodation meant that pupils no longer had to live at Froyle and travel daily to Holybourne.

The list of visits and events grew. In addition to the usual trips to France and Germany, parties from the College went to Austria, Canada and Italy as well as the Joytown Special School in Kenya. A sponsored marathon on May Day raised money to buy a minibus for the latter, and Princess Anne visited the Riding for the Disabled Group in Medstead and talked to the pupils who were there. The visit to Churchtown Farm in Cornwall by the Fourth Form became an annual fixture.

Treloar's had several musical pupils who took and passed various exams for flute, recorder and piano as well as singing. In December 1983 the first of the Glaziers' Company Concerts was given after the Master of the Glaziers invited the College to give a Christmas concert at their Hall in London. This was so successful that it became a biennial event.

In the mid-1980s it was apparent that full-time employment for College leavers was becoming increasingly difficult. The main reasons were the economic climate in the country and the greater degree of disability of many of the students. It was decided to try to help them 'acquire a skill which could be used positively after leaving the College—be it in full-time open employment, in a sheltered work environment, as a money making venture working from home or merely as a leisure [activity] providing stimulation in an otherwise housebound life.' For this, a Vocational Skills Centre was needed at the Upper School and Sir Alan Traill, Lord Mayor of London, launched the appeal at the start of his mayoral year in November 1984. Building started on the Traill Centre in September 1985.

At the same time, the Skinners' and Merchant Taylors' Companies decided to celebrate the quincentenary of the Billesden Award (the arbitration by Lord Mayor Billesden in 1484 as to their order of precedence as livery companies) by establishing an endowment fund for Treloar's. The money was to be used to employ a 'Billesden officer' at the College who would keep in touch with former students after they left and use the feedback to improve the curriculum for those coming after.

Sixth Form students were already studying for BTEC, RSA and City and Guilds qualifications in Typewriting, Amenity Horticulture, Art and Design and Commercial Subjects, and each of the pupils on the Business Technology Course spent a week in the Appeals Office at Froyle to give them work experience. By 1985 the Sixth Form contained nearly 90 pupils, some of whom were working towards the Certificate of Pre-Vocational Education.

99   *The Duchess of Gloucester chatting to students.*

100   *Prince Charles visiting Physio, 25 March 1987.*

November 1986 saw a team from Treloar's reach the final of the radio quiz show 'Top of the Form'. This was to be the last programme of the 38-year run and it was broadcast on 1 December. Ryan Cheal, Juliet Boyd, Clare Walker and Ben Hardie (who replaced Kathy MacKay) were narrowly beaten by Christ College, Brecon. A few months before this, the *Daily Mirror* had printed a list of the 'ten most expensive schools in Britain' and, at £12,198 a year, Lord Mayor Treloar College came at the top, beating Worcester College for the Blind, Harrow and Winchester College. Eton did not even appear in the list!

On 25 March 1987 there was another royal visit. Prince Charles came to open the Traill Centre at Holybourne. Pupils from the Lower School were not left out and they entertained the Prince with music and songs. There followed a tour round various classrooms and therapy before the Prince performed the opening ceremony. As he left by helicopter, the Prince (and the assembled crowds) were entertained by a bagpipe duet from the Headmaster and the Trust Accountant.

Due to bad weather, the Prince had travelled to Holybourne by car and not helicopter. Two days later the weather got worse and, as recorded in the 1987 College Magazine:

there was a near catastrophe in the Lower School Physio Department. We were in the Typing Room, the wind was gusting 45 mph. I was looking for something to type when there was a strange noise and I looked up just in time to see the roof of the staffroom, physio department, 1m and 1a classrooms lift up. Panic filled me as the roof headed towards us, but we were saved by the old beech tree which stopped the charging roof in its tracks.

In the autumn, the weather caused more problems. The Headmaster wrote to parents on 20 October saying:

nobody in the College was hurt when the hurricane swept across Hampshire on the morning of 16th October, but many buildings sustained minor damage and a large number of trees in the grounds were blown down or severely damaged. The Lower School had both water and electricity cut off which made living conditions difficult for both pupils and staff and therefore all pupils present on Saturday 17th October were transferred to the Upper School where accommodation was arranged for them.

The usual half-term Parents-Teachers-Therapists Meeting was postponed.

101 *Prince Charles talking to staff.*

102   *The College float ready for the Lord Mayor's Show, November 1987.*

The opening of the Traill Centre encouraged more applications for post-16 places, and in 1987 there were 118 students in the Sixth Form. This again put pressure on the houses and it was decided to add a wing to Allen House to provide more ground-floor study bedrooms. The appeal for this was by one of the three charities supported by the Lord Mayor, Sir Greville Spratt, during his year of office. Because of this, Treloar's entered a float in the Lord Mayor's Show which took place on 14 November.

At the Lower School there had also been developments. The Annual Report for 1987 explained:

> Conductive Education—the holistic approach to teaching and developing certain types of handicapped children, which was pioneered at the Peto Institute in Hungary—has received considerable publicity recently. Under the direction of Mrs Perks, the Head Therapist, a special course has been developed at the College, based on the Peto principles, which we have called FLAME—Function, Language and Movement Education.

The scheme began with two small groups of pupils about 11 years old. The aim was to increase motivation and confidence and improve balance.

By 1988, it was realised that, while pupil numbers remained high at 285, there were far more applications for post-16 places than for school-age ones. It was therefore decided that Froyle would, in the future, cater for pupils up to 16 years old and hence become, for the first time, an examination centre for the new GCSEs. Plans were drawn up for improving facilities, including a Craft, Design and Technology teaching area, support facilities for Computer Studies, interview rooms, an additional Science Laboratory and a new Medical Centre. It was planned to convert the Oast House into the Craft, Design and Technology and Art rooms with a Photographic Studio and accommodation for Housemasters and other staff. A new Medical Centre was to be built in part of the horticultural area allowing the existing Centre to be converted into extra classrooms and offices.

In the grounds at Froyle, the Royal Engineers Junior Leaders Regiment constructed an adventure playground, completing it in only five days. Across the A31, the pond used for fishing had been restocked. The biggest carp had been netted, sold and replaced by 100 tench. Pupils were also catching perch, roach and rudd.

In September a joint team from the College and Lord Wandsworth College reached the final of the British Telecom Kielder Challenge in Northumberland. They came third out of the 50 teams entered. Even more adventurous trips were to follow—a week's skiing at Gstaad and a walking/climbing expedition to the Lake District.

103   *The Oast House after conversion.*

104   *The visit of Princess Diana, 23 January 1989.*

The autumn of 1988 marked the 80th Anniversary of the opening of the College and, on 23 January 1989, the Princess of Wales paid a visit to Froyle. She managed to visit every part of the School, including the Newton-Davis Hall, where students from Holybourne were showing work from their courses. The events of the Anniversary Year were published in the booklet *80 Summers on.*

In the summer of 1989 Mr Maitland retired as Head of the Lower School after seeing Froyle through its change from a boys' college to a mixed school. His place was taken by Neil Clark, who came from Keswick School in Cumbria.

In October 1989 the BBC's 'Children in Need' campaign donated £20,000 to enable the launch of 'IMPact'. This was an initiative of the therapists to provide students with a thorough assessment and some financial help towards the purchase of their own wheelchairs. However, fundraising was not all one way. The students at Treloar's had, for a long time, raised money for others with events such as Marathon Day and Red Nose Day, and this tradition continues.

January 1990 saw the School featured on the television programme 'Jim'll Fix It'. It all began when two pupils wrote a letter about a teacher, Hugh Terry, and his watch. He was always telling them that with his watch he could contact the pilots of the helicopters that often flew over Froyle. The pupils asked for the programme to arrange for a real helicopter to land one day. There was a problem though—how would the pilots know when to come? It was then decided to turn things around. Filming started in July 1989 and the pupils were told it was for an educational documentary. The helicopter arrived on cue and whisked Mr Terry off to sit by a swimming pool and be served a Kir Royale at a luxury hotel! Pupils and teacher later went to the television studios for the rest of the filming and Mr Terry was awarded his 'Jim'll Fix It' badge.

On 25 January 1990 another storm hit the area. Holybourne was without power for about a day and a half and this meant a supper of soup and sandwiches. As before, Froyle suffered worse, losing water as well as power. The Lower School pupils who could not get home were again transferred to Holybourne.

At the end of the summer term 1990, Mr Macpherson retired after 16 years as Headmaster. As he wrote in the College Magazine, 'Wheels '90':

> In 1974 when I started work at Froyle my first impressions were of horror and apprehension for what I had taken on. The Governors told me that I had two main jobs to do. First of all, the staff had to be kept under control. Secondly, the boys were uncouth, ill mannered and disobedient and it was essential to introduce some discipline to the school; furthermore I had to put an end to what they got up to with toothpaste … There were no Houseparents, no Classroom Assistants, no Occupational Therapists, no Speech Therapists (there was a part-time Physio), no Medical Officer, no Deputy Head, no Senior Master, no Senior Mistress, and NO GIRLS.

105 *'Jim'll Fix It'.*

106   *Mr and Mrs Macpherson leaving Treloar's, 1990.*

Mr Macpherson was subsequently awarded an OBE for his services to Treloar's.

The new Headmaster was Hartley Heard, who came from the Royal Grammar School, Guildford. Another new member of staff joining at this time was the Rev. Roger Royle, the broadcaster, who became College Chaplain. He was appointed to take the place of Treloar's first Chaplain, the Rev. Richard Avery, who had recently died.

Students at the Upper School continued to travel far and wide. In May 1991 a group went on an exchange trip to Russia. They were based at the Demitrov School near Moscow and visited the Kremlin, Lenin's Tomb, the Old Moscow Circus and the Winter Palace in Leningrad. Other parties went to Denmark, Germany, Holland, Florida and Churchtown Farm. In the next few years there were visits to Ireland and Stackpole in Wales. Teams and individuals also travelled to various sporting events such as the National Junior Archery competition at Rugby, the National Junior Athletics Championships at Blackpool, the National Junior Basketball Championships at Stoke Mandeville and the National Junior Swimming Championships at Darlington. Jamie Wood went to Australia as part of the British Paraplegic Team to compete in the javelin, shot and discus events.

For those who were stage-struck there had been many performances over the years, including 'My Fair Lady', 'Quest of Heroes', 'West Side Story', 'Toad of Toad Hall', 'Bugsy Malone', 'Cyrano de Bergerac' and 'Joe Carpenter and Son'. Excerpts from some of these productions were performed as part of the biennial concerts at the Glaziers' Hall in London.

Mr Chris Williams, who was in charge of the catering on both sites, was interviewed by the students for the Autumn 1991 issue of *The Treloar Times*. He revealed that there were 55 catering staff at both the Upper and Lower Schools and that they worked in shifts from 7 a.m. to 8 p.m. When Prince Charles came, 'there was a security guard stationed in the kitchen to test all the food as it was to be served'. In a survey, it seemed that the students' favourite lunch was fish and chips followed by gateau.

107 *College students visiting Russia, May 1991.*

During the early 1990s the country was in recession and the government 'capped' local authorities' expenditure. Due to this and the increased integration of disabled pupils into state schools, there was a sudden drop in numbers of new students for September 1992. Faced with a deficit of about £1 million in the budget, the Trustees were forced to make cutbacks and, as salaries were the biggest expenditure, this meant shedding some 15 per cent of posts. It was hoped that much of this could be achieved by natural wastage and early retirement, but there were a few redundancies and Gauvain House, at Holybourne, was closed.

108 *'Cyrano de Bergerac'.*

109   *The running track at Holybourne.*

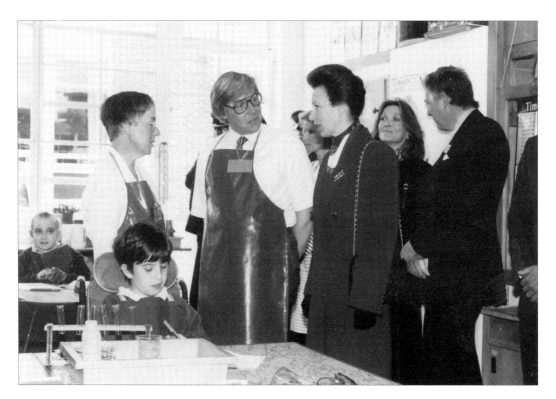

110   *Visit of the Princess Royal, 1997.*

At the same time, the Upper School at Holybourne began to take on the ethos of a Further Education College and was selected as one of 100 establishments in the country to pilot the new General National Vocational Qualifications (GNVQs). The School at Froyle also had something new to address—the National Curriculum. Making it accessible to Treloar pupils proved challenging.

1993 saw the establishment of Treloar Enterprises Limited as the Trust's trading company. Tax and VAT rules limited the extent to which a charity could trade and so this took on all peripheral activities of Treloar's, such as the hiring out of the premises and the rehabilitation engineering services.

The demand for places at Froyle and Holybourne began to increase. Evans House was enlarged and redesigned, and Gauvain House was re-opened after major improvements. A Retreat/Chapel and a Wheelchair Assessment Centre were created at Holybourne, the swimming pool was refurbished and a self-service cafeteria was introduced.

Froyle Place, which had accommodated students since the move from the Hospital in the early 1950s, could no longer be adapted to take the increasing number of wheelchairs and pupils with complex needs. It was decided to build a new 48-bed house for the youngest children on the site of the tennis courts. An appeal was launched in 1995 and the necessary £2.6 million was raised in 18 months. Named Heywood House, after the first Warden of Froyle, it was completed in September 1996 and officially opened by the Princess Royal on 8 May 1997.

Over the years, the complexity and types of disability among the students gradually changed. The number of haemophiliacs and those with spina bifida decreased while more students with cerebral palsy and Duchenne muscular dystrophy joined Treloar's. A growing number of pupils were joint-funded by the local education authorities, social services and health authorities.

The creation of the Further Education Funding Council (FEFC) in 1992 to oversee all post-16 education was the catalyst for a major restructuring when the Trustees decided to split the School and College. On 1 April 1995 the Department of Education approved the Froyle site as a Non-Maintained Special School for pupils aged five to 16 and it was renamed Lord Mayor Treloar School. At the same time, the Holybourne site became a National Specialist College for Further Education for those from 16 to 25, with placement and funding of almost all students coming under the FEFC. The College now offered GNVQ, NVQ, City and Guilds, RSA and Pitman courses as well as the ASDAN Youth Awards, GCSEs and GCE A Levels, and the relationship with Alton Sixth Form College thrived.

Sport continued to play an important part in the life of School and College. Several members of the Junior Swimming Team were chosen as part of the English team for a match against other European countries and America. The Head of P.E., Morag McGlashan, was appointed as a coach to the British disabled swimming squad and Ryan Gratrix represented Great Britain in an international event in Bratislava, Slovakia. Ryan and Vicki Broadribb were members of the Paralympic team that went to Atlanta in 1996. Rebecca Gale, a

111   *The track at Froyle with Heywood House in the background.*

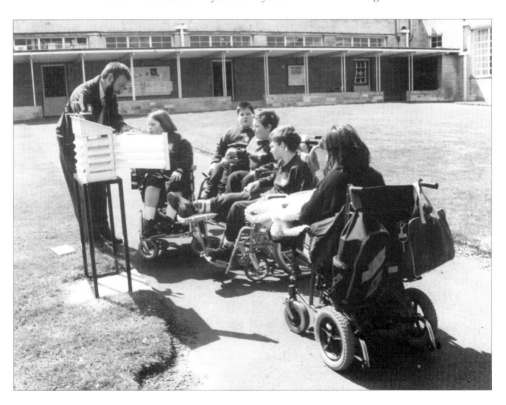

112   *A Geography lesson at Froyle.*

former student, represented Great Britain in archery and both she and Vicky won bronze medals. After leaving Treloar's, Vicki went on to win a gold medal at the European Swimming Championships at the same time that Danielle Watts won three gold medals and broke three world records. Both Vicki and Danielle competed in the 2000 Paralympics in Sydney, with Vicki winning a gold medal and later being awarded the MBE.

The last few years of the millennium saw several staff changes. Dr Jane Lones retired after 25 years at Treloar's. Having started teaching Science at the Florence Treloar School, becoming Head of Science and Senior Mistress, she was then made Head of the Upper School at Holybourne. Her place was taken by Dr Graham Jowett who had previously been Manager at Crawley College, West Sussex.

The summer of 1996 also saw the departure of Iain Young, who had been the College's Senior Master. As he recalled in an interview before he left, his most embarrassing moment was being arrested by the local police and locked in a cell one Red Nose Day. He was kept there one hour for every £10 raised by the students, and would have stayed there for seven hours had the staff not taken pity on him and made a collection to have him released earlier. John Smith, who had taught College pupils to drive for 13 years, retired in the same year but, unable to stay away, he returned to assist in the Performing Arts class.

113   *Iain Young locked up on Red Nose Day.*

114   *Cooking and ironing in one of the Independent Living Flats at Holybourne.*

The next year there were changes in the senior management of the Trust. Mr Heard moved on to become Principal of Doncaster College for the Deaf and Colonel John Sweeting, who had been the Bursar, became the Trust's first Chief Executive. Separate governing bodies were appointed, with Bruce Powell and Alastair Graham being the first Chairmen for the School and College respectively, while Michael Campbell, who had succeeded General Sir David Fraser in 1993, remained as Trust Chairman. Neil Clark, as Headteacher of the School, and Graham Jowett, as Principal of the College, assumed full responsibility for their establishments and reported directly to their respective Chairmen.

After years of having adapted coaches for transporting students, the Trust took delivery of a new coach specially designed to its own requirements in the academic year 1998-9. The cost was £140,000, with the exterior colour scheme being the subject of an in-house competition. Treloar transport covers thousands of miles a year, including taking students to sporting events all over the country. Some of these were to play Boccia (a version of boules), and all the hard work of students and staff was rewarded when David Morgan represented Great Britain in Argentina and Amy Bishop and Cecilia Turk became National Champions.

The millennium saw several visits to the Millennium Dome and the School's own 'Lord Mayor's Show'—depicting the history of Treloar's. The College put on an 'Arts Week' which included music, dance, pantomime and poetry. In

April the College's new Marjorie Gill Horticultural Centre was opened by Alan Titchmarsh, the broadcaster, and in June Lt Gen. Sir Hew Pike opened the new Pike House at the School. Another new facility was the Learning Resource Centre at the College, which housed a new library, I.T. classrooms and staff training rooms. These projects were followed by the building of Campbell Court (seven flats for Independent Living) at Holybourne and a new kitchen and dining room complex at Froyle.

There are so many things now on offer at Treloar's that Sir William Treloar could never have imagined but of which he would surely have approved. Every student has a dedicated computer—many of which have been specially adapted by the rehabilitation engineers with advice from the occupational therapists. Both the School and College have a team of physiotherapists and speech and language and occupational therapists on site. As well as attending to students' physical needs, they offer the chance to work on domestic and community skills. Many students have speech, language or hearing difficulties, and advice and support is given on suitable communication aids.

The living accommodation is a very far cry from the pitched pine Army buildings that were in use for the first years of Treloar's history. Each house is now divided into small units which makes the atmosphere less institutional. Gone are the rows of dormitory beds—replaced by small individual or shared rooms that students can personalise with pictures and posters.

115   *The Rev. Ed Pruen and friends.*

Many of the jobs of the 700 staff would be familiar to Sir William—the gardeners, porters, teachers and nurses. Some, though, he would not recognise—educational psychologists, dieticians, counsellors and visual-impairment advisors. Treloar's now has its own full-time Chaplain, the Rev. Ed Pruen, and the students no longer have to do the 'housekeeping' themselves. The fundraising and administrative aspects of the Trust are all now housed in Froyle and have to raise much more than the £15,000 a year that was needed 'to keep Alton going' in 1911.

Despite there being so many facets to Treloar's, it has never been forgotten that the main purpose of Treloar's since 1948 is education in its broadest sense. So it may be said, 100 years after Sir William Treloar's Hospital and College first opened its doors, that Treloar's is still providing 'a sound education'.

116   *The Treloar coat of arms.*

Index

References in **bold** type are to illustrations.